THE
FAITH
DARE

Also by Debbie Alsdorf

Deeper
A Different Kind of Wild

THE FAITH DARE

30 Days to Live Your Life to the Fullest

DEBBIE ALSDORF

Revell

a division of Baker Publishing Group
Grand Rapids, Michigan

Published by Revell
a division of Baker Publishing Group
P.O. Box 6287, Grand Rapids, MI 49516-6287
www.revellbooks.com

Printed in the United States of America

Library of Congress Cataloging-in-Publication Data
Alsdorf, Debbie.
    The faith dare : 30 days to live your life to the fullest / Debbie Alsdorf.
      p. cm.
    Includes bibliographical references.
    ISBN 978-0-8007-3367-4 (pbk.)
    1. Christian women—Religious life. 2. Christian women—Prayers and devo-
tions. 3. Spirituality. I. Title.
    BV4527.A458 2010
    242′.643—dc22   2010009650

In keeping with biblical principles of creation stewardship, Baker Publishing Group advocates the responsible use of our natural resources. As a member of the Green Press Initiative, our company uses recycled paper when possible. The text paper of this book is comprised of 30% post-consumer waste.

green press INITIATIVE

16   7 6

This book is for all the women, like myself, who want something more, something real, and a faith that changes the ordinary moments into an extraordinary journey with God.

I dedicate *The Faith Dare* to two special women who have consistently dared me—challenging me to live biblically:

Liz Grundvig, who for years has pointed me in the direction of faith, in her no-nonsense way of challenging me to live for my heavenly Father and in accordance with biblical truth.

Eileen Terpstra, who is like a spiritual compass in my life, encouraging me to line up my life with God and daring me to live out my faith in real life, no matter how hard it is.

This faith is the firm foundation
under everything that makes life
worth living.

Hebrews 11:1 Message

Contents

Introduction

Wild Faith?

Being fully persuaded that God [has] power to do what
he [has] promised.

Romans 4:21

The Christian life is a different life—walked out with
intention, conviction, and humble surrender.

Debbie Alsdorf

I have not always been a woman of spiritual faith. Truth is I grew
up very much afraid, a child in an alcoholic home who learned how
to be nice and agreeable in the hope that life would remain calm. I
also learned how to live in perfection, performance, and pleasing
other people—and was afraid of failure, rejection, or conflict.

I learned from a young age to put my faith in myself, my performance, and other people's opinions of me. This type of faith is
the dead-end existence many Christian women are living in today.
We go to church, recite the creeds, learn the verses, sing the songs,

attend the classes—but we apply little of what we see, hear, or say we learned. We paste on our smiles and act full, when inside we are empty and unfulfilled.

This book is not about faith in ourselves. It is about faith in a God who is bigger than us, more powerful than us, and filled with more love for us than we could possibly begin to imagine. It is this God, the one who created us on purpose—for his purpose—whom we can trust with every aspect of our lives.

The problem is that trusting a God we do not see does not come naturally to us. Trusting God is a spiritual lifestyle to be learned. Walking out that faith takes a lifetime of baby steps in the direction of spiritual truth. As we grow, we learn how to trust God. We develop new habits of looking to him, new habits of processing and digesting the Word of God, new habits of living our faith, and new habits of relating to other people in our lives. New habits don't happen overnight; they happen over time.

I wasn't raised knowing about a personal relationship with Christ, but in 1973 I heard about God's love for me and became a Christian. Since then I have longed to know Jesus better and serve him more. This heart desire has been strong and sincere, but my method of reaching him has often been the same as the methods I used to cope with life before knowing him—perfection, performance, and pleasing others. I learned to be a good rule keeper but was not spiritually alive. In many ways I was dead inside, and for years I dealt with a secret low-grade depression that kept me believing my life's glass was chronically half empty, when in reality it was full. I could not see the goodness of God because I could not see past myself. I wish it were not so, but that is the truth of my story.

This type of Christian life breeds competition with other people, jealousies, and judging, and these play out in every evil work. "For where you have envy and selfish ambition, there you find disorder and every evil practice" (James 3:16). This is the opposite of the life of grace and faith that Jesus calls abundance. But it was my natural default caused by a fear of not being enough, being left out, or having to prove myself. Many women have told me they can relate to all of the above and want a different life too.

Little did I know that it would take the breaking of all that I loved to bring me to the point of depression and emptiness of soul that would lead me to a path of renewed surrender to the God who made me—this same God I had been calling Lord for many years.

The past twenty years of my life have been a journey into something deeper, a ride of wild faith that has taken me places I had never dreamed of, has tested everything I ever thought or believed. The end result has left me with one thought: God is true, mighty, and loving. This thought is what guides me on the path of faith today.

I describe this new path as wild because it is wildly different from anything I have ever known. It is uncharted terrain for me. It is not conventional, not understandable, but radical. I also like to think of wild as being an acronym: Woman In Lifelong Development. When I focus on God's process of developing me and shaping me in faith, I get excited. When I focus on the process, I am okay letting go of the perfection. When I focus on the process of development, my life falls into a new groove. Maybe it's like the groove spoken about in Psalm 84:

> Blessed are those whose strength is in you,
>   who have set their hearts on pilgrimage.
> As they pass through the Valley of Baca,
>   they make it a place of springs. . . .
> They go from strength to strength
>   till each appears before God.
>
> vv. 5–7

What I Am Learning

As God takes me through this process, I am learning some important lessons.

11

- I have to let go of self-strength, self-effort, and trusting anything of self. I am still learning.

- I have to set my heart on the pilgrimage, which is an extended journey with a purpose. This is what God's Word calls our life! And I have to set my heart and mind on faith in God for the journey, the life he purposed for me alone.

- I have to accept the valleys and desert places and choose to embrace them and trust God in them. I am learning that embracing these places and trusting God in them are what makes them a place of springs. The outcome of our faith is not only pleasing to God but also a benefit to us. We begin to leap from faith to faith, peace to peace, joy to joy—no matter what our circumstances.

My dear friend Sheree says it this way: "I refuse to be defined by my circumstances." This is a statement of what faith is to me. Rather than be defined by my stuff, I will let the truth of God's Word define me, direct my choices, and get me in a faith groove. I am still choosing this groove on a daily basis. Some days are easier than others. I am growing, learning, and developing. And that is what this thirty-day challenge is all about. It's like setting thirty days aside for a reboot, so we can be refreshed and have more energy for the journey ahead.

Rebooting a computer returns the software and hardware to their initial state, which in theory should eliminate problems. Has your computer ever frozen for no apparent reason? Nothing you do makes a difference. It's like some programming somewhere deep inside is stuck and will not resolve itself until it is powered down and the computer is rebooted.

Sometimes it seems as though my life operating system is frozen. I get stuck, and I know things will not change until I power down from "self" and restart with the power of the Holy Spirit.

The thirty-day challenge in this book is about daring to walk further away from self and move closer to God and his wisdom, truth, and power. Let's face it, life often looks like the Valley of Baca, the desert place, but even in that place we can splash in springs of faith, which lead us to the abundance of life Jesus came to give us.

Do you want your fullest life? It begins with faith.

Wild faith is surrendered, passionate, and courageous. It humbly seeks and fearlessly follows. Most of us only dream about wild faith. We live a repressed, suppressed, depressed type of faith. It's time to live in all that God has for us. It's time to live our fullest, richest, most abundant life—a life of walking, breathing, eating, sleeping *faith*.

Here's to thirty days of challenging our beliefs and daring to follow the truth!

The Habit of a Focused Heart

The heart is the center of who we are. Often we are not interested in this center place and instead work on the exterior places we can see. But the heart itself leads the parade of all exterior activity. All life and action flow out of what is in the heart, the center of a person. Because of this, it is important to pay attention to the condition and health of this center place. Is Christ dwelling in your heart by faith? Or are other things crowding out the life and love of Christ? Becoming intentional about our heart condition is important and will keep us from hardened hearts that are not able to hear God and be moved by him.

In his work *Bringing Sons unto Glory*, Oswald Chambers said:

> When a man's heart is right with God the mysterious utterances of the Bible are spirit and life to him. Spiritual truth is discernible only to a pure heart, not to a keen intellect. It is not a question of profundity or intellect, but of purity of heart.[1]

We pay so little attention to the habits of our heart. In the next thirty days you'll examine the thoughts, intent, and reaction of your heart, looking at how you view life and what Scripture says about the path to the fullest life. You will begin a new habit of looking *up* more than you did before—looking up to truth, looking up to God, looking up for help, looking up for understanding, looking up for wisdom, and looking up for forgiveness, grace, and cleansing.

We spend so much time trying to look good on the outside. Image is everything, or so the ads promise. In our quest to get our stuff together we take classes on organizing our clutter, revamping our wardrobe, or perfecting our makeup. These are all externals. In the next thirty days you'll concentrate on organizing the inside places, areas that have been disordered, hidden from view, and affect the way you live. This will be the beginning of developing holy habits of the interior world, habits that over time will be second nature because the life change has become a part of us as we have learned to connect intimately with the Father.

It takes thirty days to form a habit. Repeat anything consistently, and it begins to form a groove or a pattern in you. In time our habits become a natural part of us, and we do the things we used to have to think about doing without much thought. Most of us forget to make the things of the spiritual life part of our new habit patterns. We assume they will happen by osmosis, but they will not. Just like your frozen computer needs to be rebooted, the spiritual part of you needs to be turned off from self and restarted in a new habit of living up to God. The more we learn to focus on God, the more we learn to look up and live up. This is when life gets exciting and our experience with God comes to the place of abundance.

Some of these thirty days will be more of a challenge than the others. Follow the dare for each day, stretching yourself even if you think you don't need help in that area. None of us is perfect, and we all need continual spiritual direction.

If you are challenged by one of the days in particular, stay with that dare a little longer. You are not in a rush to be spiritual in thirty days flat! It's not about finishing the book, it's about changing and finishing strong. It's about becoming a new woman living the life God has planned for you as his daughter. You are already spiritual, as God's Spirit resides inside you. Now is the time to get into the habit of remembering *who* you are and *whose* you are—daring yourself to quit operating by the world's systems and turn instead to the original operating system of God's Word.

Making the Most of This Book

By now you have figured out that this book was not written for casual entertainment. It was written for life change and personal application. It was written for action!

The central focus is the thirty-day faith dare, which is a "fasting of self." To fast is to deny ourselves something—food, drink, media, pleasure. A fast creates a space for seeking God and hearing from him. Scripture outlines promises associated with fasting.

> Is not this the kind of fasting I have chosen: . . .
> to set the oppressed free
>   and break every yoke?
> Then your light will break forth like the dawn,
>   and your healing will quickly appear;
> then your righteousness will go before you,
>   and the glory of the LORD will be your rear guard.
> Then you will call, and the LORD will answer;
>   you will cry for help and he will say: Here am I.
>
> Isaiah 58:6, 8–9

I am challenging you to a fasting of self. For thirty days you will be placing your self and what you want to do aside, replacing them with the truths in each day's dare, and concentrating on what God is saying to your heart that day. I want you to begin to see how God meets you in this place of surrendered focus on him. I want you to be not only blessed by his presence but also addicted to the

15

abundance of peace and serenity that comes from believing God is who he says he is.

The daily readings will help you practice looking *up* to God, looking *in* at your heart and attitudes, and living *out* your faith in practical ways. The goal is to build a habit of centering on God one day at a time. My prayer is that after the thirty days are completed, you will long for more—more of living from a focused center, less focused on self and more focused on how God is leading you through his Word, through your interior response to his Word, and through practical application of his Word.

Part 1 helps you prepare your heart for the faith dare by looking at what faith is and why it is important for us to develop a life of faith. Don't skip this section. Read it, think about it, allow it to prepare you for what's to come.

The Thirty-Day Faith Dare

You are encouraged to set aside a time daily, preferably at the beginning of the day, to read that day's truth and dare. It is helpful if you can find a time when you are not distracted, can focus for a short time, and can process what you are reading. After you have read and processed the truth, you will have the opportunity to jot down your immediate thoughts. After you are done, take the dare into your day and intentionally apply that truth and your own personal dare to your life. Make a mental note of how this made that day different, or journal during the thirty days about how God is changing your life through this fasting of self and intentional focus on him and his Word.

Read one section each day, as the thirty-day faith dare guides you down a path of focusing on God and the truth of his Word. Here is the format:

- Today's Praise/Prayer: Try reading the psalm out loud; this will help you gain focus. If you cannot read it out loud, then read it slowly with focus and with an attitude of opening your heart for the truth that will come next.

- Today's Truth: These verses on the daily subject verify the importance of taking a focused look up to God and an intentional look at how God's truth might be different from things we tend to believe. It will be important to "sit" with the truth in each day's Scripture. Think about the truth, rehearse the truth in your mind, memorize the truth, and ask God to show you what you need to know about that day's truth. Allow it to challenge you to action.

- Today's Dare: This section contains a dare and some questions or applications concerning how to practice the truth in a way that challenges you and dares you to step out further in your faith walk.

- Journal: Here you will have a chance to jot down thoughts that come to your heart and mind as you begin to process the subject of the day and dare yourself to walk in faith.

- Today's Prayer: If you're new to prayer, these words will help you begin. Follow your heart as God leads you. Each day begins with looking up through the praise/prayer and ends with looking up with a prayer to God for direction, life change, help to complete the dare, and thanksgiving for who he is.

- Today I Believe: This section contains a final truth affirmation for the day.

Doing the Dare with a Group

Typically women like to do things with their friends. We go on diets together, go on walks together, shop and hang out together. Doing life together is a wonderful aspect of community talked about throughout the New Testament and specifically in the book of Acts. Doing the thirty-day dare in this type of community life is rewarding and provides accountability. Together you will share stories of new choices, attitude change, and seeing God at work in your midst. You will share tales of experiencing his presence when you pray instead of worry. With such personal excitement for the truth, you will help everyone in the group grow. Together everyone achieves more!

If you are doing the thirty-day dare with a group, here is a suggested schedule:

1. Read part 1. Come together with your group and discuss how you personally are preparing for the thirty days and what you hope to receive from the thirty-day faith dare. Pray for strength, focus, and for God to be pleased as you put your hope and faith in him alone.
2. Begin the thirty-day challenge. You can begin a blog to keep everyone accountable on that day's subject matter. You may also want to use the technology of Twitter to keep tabs on each other's process (more on how to do both in the following section). Or you may want to pair off into accountability partners.
3. After the thirty-day dare, come together to tell your stories of how God challenged you to stretch your faith as you dared to live it out. This is a time to encourage one another.
4. Commit to a future plan of looking up to God and living out of faith when it's more natural to look down and live in the flesh.

Twitter, Blogs, and Other Technical Tools for Connecting

"Do you tweet?" a woman at a conference asked me. I was confused. Did I look like a bird? Was I missing something? I soon learned about Twitter, and it could be a fun way to keep in touch with your small group during the thirty-day dare.

18

A tweet is a message posted on Twitter. It is easy to get a free Twitter account. Here is what Wikipedia has to say about this technology:

> Twitter is a free social networking and micro-blogging service that enables its users to send and read messages known as *tweets*. Tweets are text-based posts of up to 140 characters displayed on the author's profile page and delivered to the author's subscribers who are known as *followers*. Senders can restrict delivery to those in their circle of friends or, by default, allow open access. Users can send and receive tweets via the Twitter website, Short Message Service (SMS) or external applications. While the service, itself, costs nothing to use, accessing it through SMS may incur phone service provider fees.[2]

To get your own Twitter account you can google Twitter or go to twitter.com for step-by-step instructions. It really is very easy. I have it on my phone as well, using a phone application (for which I paid a small amount) called Tweetie.

Blogging is also gaining popularity by the day. If I can set up a blog all by myself, trust me, so can you. Let's again turn to Wikipedia for a clear description of a blog:

> A blog (a contraction of the term "web log") is a type of website, usually maintained by an individual with regular entries of commentary, descriptions of events, or other material such as graphics or video. Entries are commonly displayed in reverse-chronological order. "Blog" can also be used as a verb, meaning *to maintain or add content to a blog.*
>
> Many blogs provide commentary or news on a particular subject; others function as more personal online diaries. A typical blog combines text, images, and links to other blogs, Web pages, and other media related to its topic. The ability for readers to leave comments in an interactive format is an important part of many blogs. Most blogs are primarily textual, although some focus on

art (artlog), photographs (photoblog), sketches (sketchblog), videos (vlog), music (MP3 blog), and audio (podcasting). Micro-blogging is another type of blogging, featuring very short posts.[3]

I began blogging by googling blog and finding blogspot.com, which is a free blogging site. I quickly was able to set up a blog with the easy step-by-step instructions. Once you set it up and let people know, a community is formed!

Whatever you do as a group, be committed to daring yourself each day to walk further away from the way you do things and closer to the way Scripture teaches us to walk in the Spirit—living in relationship with God, a relationship of spiritual responsibility with self, and a relationship of love toward others.

Let's Begin Our Reboot!

- Power down from self—come to Christ daily.
- Restart in the power of the Spirit—follow him daily.
- Open up to new possibilities—experience the difference he makes in a surrendered life.

Important Things
for the Thirty-Day Journey

Cling to your faith in Christ, and keep your conscience clear. For some people have deliberately violated their consciences; as a result, their faith has been shipwrecked.

1 Timothy 1:19 NLT

1

Faith Defined

What Is It and Why Is It Important?

Accepting Christ changed my life—embracing faith
changes the way I live.

Christy Harper

All of us put our faith in something or someone. To say you don't
have faith is to say you don't have life. Just think of the car you
drive. You have faith that it will get you where you are going. You
don't see the inner working of the engine; you just have faith that it
is working. You put your trust in it. What about the foods we eat?
We trust that they will not make us sick. In today's environment
that takes faith! Whenever we can't see something but we believe it
will fulfill its promised or intended purpose, that constitutes faith.
The Webster's Dictionary defines faith as belief in the truth, value,
or trustworthiness of someone or something; loyalty or allegiance;
belief or trust in God.

Each of us has developed habits concerning whom or what we put our faith in. Many of us, even well-meaning Christians, have learned to put our faith in human wisdom and human understanding. We have developed ingrained habits of thinking, reasoning, and living that have become part of us through repetition and practice. When it comes to our spiritual lives, we have habits of thinking, reacting, believing, and living that often keep us from God's intended best for us.

If you want more—the fullest life possible—you must learn to focus on what is true according to God's Word: the claims of Christ, the promises of Christ, and the character of Christ. This focus is not natural for us because we grow up learning to focus on ourselves. But this upward focus can become our new normal and change us in ways we never thought possible.

This focus can change your life. You will have a new foundation for living. While most of us are worried about our appearance and lifting something besides our sagging faith, what really matters and what we really need is a faith lift—an upward lifting of our eyes to God, every day, many times a day.

Just this morning I got a facebook message from a woman I haven't seen in a while. She said, "Debbie, I seem to have run out of hope. I haven't been to church in a year! I am broken and angry! Where do I go from here? Is there a twelve-step program or something to help me have faith again?"

What do you think is going on with this woman? She obviously has been hurt or encountered hard times. She might even be hurt that God hasn't pulled through for her. Or she might be living in her old lifestyle again, leaving her exasperated and discouraged about her ability to find God or live in him. Most importantly, she wants to recover from "self" and be restored in her relationship with God.

I could relate to this woman because many times I have felt faithless and frustrated. I have been angry at God and at others whom I thought had the power to fix my life, or at least help it out a bit. I too have often wondered why there wasn't a recovery program for people like me—someone who needed to recover from the dysfunction of having been a Christian for years but never having learned how to trust God! For me the excuses had to end. I wanted everything and anything God had laid out for me. And to get that I had to lay down my way and learn to live in his. I can't believe how hard it is to keep realigning my thoughts, my speech, and my attitude. But I want God's best. Do you?

It still surprises me how many verses and principles I have learned over the years that I have not once tried to live out in my daily life. In the past I wouldn't have admitted it, but now I am open about this reality because I know there are other women like me who know what God's Word says but don't dare apply it to their lives. If we don't apply God's Word, we will not experience the fullness of life God came to give us. It's like knowing the calories in a chocolate éclair but eating it anyway. The results depend on what we do, not what we thought about. In the same way faith without works or action is dead. I am tired of dead faith! I would rather cultivate the faith of one tiny mustard seed than live in the deadness of a faith that is theory only.

Faith sounds theological or fanatical. It sounds like something a seminary professor should think about, not me. But recently I have been discovering how little faith I have at times and how my unbelief affects the choices I make and the way I live. More importantly, I am seeing clearly how without faith I have no chance of living a life pleasing to God. Ouch! I don't like that a bit. We can't please God the way we please other people. He isn't interested in our appearance. He is all about the heart and whether we trust him. That is why it is so important to look at what faith is, grow in an understanding of its importance, and seek to live a life of faith that is pleasing to the God who made us.

As with all things spiritual, my opinion doesn't count for much, so we need to go straight to the Word of God, which is God-breathed and useful for teaching, correcting, and training us for the spiritual journey (see 2 Timothy 3:16). The Word of God equips us for every good thing God has prepared for us to do. The Word of God is powerful and cuts into the deepest parts of us, doing for us what we could never do for ourselves (see Hebrews 4:12).

Faith Basics

The eleventh chapter of Hebrews is all about faith. This chapter outlines what faith is, explains why it is important, and provides examples of people who walked in faith.

Hebrews 11:1 tells us what faith is.

> Now faith is being sure of what we hope for and certain of what we do not see.

> What is faith? It is the confident assurance that something we want is going to happen. It is the certainty that what we hope for is waiting for us, even though we cannot see it up ahead.

> TLB

> The fundamental fact of existence is that this trust in God, this faith, is the firm foundation under everything that makes life worth living. It's our handle on what we can't see.

> Message

> Now faith is the assurance (the confirmation, the title deed) of the things [we] hope for, being the proof of things [we] do not see and the conviction of their reality [faith perceiving as real fact what is not revealed to the senses].

> AMP

Let's examine this verse so we can understand its meaning and apply it to our lives.

Faith is . . . being sure of what we hope for.

- Sure: the original Greek word is *hypostasis*, which means confidence, trust, being sure.
- Hope: the Greek word is *elpizo*, which means expect or put hope in.

Faith is . . . being certain of what we do not see.

- Certain: this is from *elenchos*, meaning proof or certainty.
- See: what I can visually see, limited by what my eyes take in.

Faith is . . . living in confident trust and certainty that God is who he says he is. It is living by what God's Word says about his ways rather than what my eyes, senses, or emotions say about each situation, circumstance, and daily challenge in this life.

Obviously we can put faith in things other than God. We can put our hope in people, in material things, in job securities. But the faith and the living proof spoken of in Hebrews is not that kind of faith. It is faith in God.

> This is what the ancients were commended for. By faith we understand that the universe was formed at God's command, so that what is seen was not made out of what was visible. By faith Abel offered God a better sacrifice than Cain did. By faith he was commended as a righteous man, when God spoke well of his offerings. And by faith he still speaks, even though he is dead.
>
> Hebrews 11:2–4

It is clear that faith in God moves us away from self and toward him. Faith in God trains us to believe in someone bigger than ourselves who can do in our lives what we cannot accomplish by ourselves. Finally, faith in God often causes us to make choices of obedience that may not make sense to us at the time but are based on what we perceive God is leading us to do through his Word and his Spirit in a given situation.

Fill in the blank. To me faith is

_____

_____

_____

_____

If faith is trusting in God, part of our problem is that we don't know what to expect from God because we don't understand God, his ways, or his love. That is why it is important to take notice of this verse: "Consequently, faith comes from hearing the message, and the message is heard through the word of Christ" (Rom. 10:17). *Faith* here is from the Greek *pistis*, which means belief. The word *message* is from *rhema*, which is a message or word from God. For us to build belief and to hear a personal message from God, we must be in the Word. When we are in the Word, we learn the ways of God, the character of God, and the love of God. The more we know him, the more we learn to trust him. Without this, we are operating on old belief systems. Without realizing it, we are putting our faith in what we have come to expect rather than in God.

A friend of mine had many bad things happen to her over the course of time. It is difficult for her to live with the assurance that history isn't going to repeat itself. She is always a little on edge, never fully trusting anything good that comes her way. Rather than expecting God to be faithful and good to her, she waits for him to zap her once again. Her life doesn't need to be a walk on eggshells, but that is how she has learned to live.

Another friend has lived her life pleasing people. Why? Because she has been rejected many times and is always waiting for someone new to reject her. This often causes her to shut down and reject others first. How can a woman learn to live in God's love when her natural bent is to protect herself from further rejection?

Both of my friends look at life in ways that have become habits for them—bad habits. There is a saying that what we know is more comfortable than what we don't know. Many of us, therefore, knowingly or unwittingly believe wrong things rather than daring to believe God is who he says he is. We desperately need a change of expectation. We need God to heal our expectations and fill our spirits. As we see God's ways, we begin to live in the joy of knowing that God is for us. We begin to view our lives and circumstances through the lens or perspective of biblical truth. God loves me, God is for me, God wants what is best for me. God can be trusted. This new way of believing produces tremendous peace!

Faith Defined: What Is It and Why Is It Important?

Take a look at what the book of Hebrews says about faith:

> And without faith it is impossible to please God, because anyone who comes to him must believe that he exists and that he rewards those who earnestly seek him.
>
> 11:6

> It's impossible to please God apart from faith. And why? Because anyone who wants to approach God must believe both that he exists and that he cares enough to respond to those who seek him.
>
> 11:6 Message

The apostle Paul writes about it in Galatians: "Am I now trying to win the approval of men, or of God? Or am I trying to please men? If I were still trying to please men, I would not be a servant of Christ" (Gal. 1:10).

I see another definition of faith emerging:

- Faith is believing God exists.

29

- Faith is believing he cares and responds to those who seek him.
- Faith is believing in and hoping in something we cannot see.
- Faith in God is believing that God indeed exists and rewards those who seek him.
- Faith in God is believing he is who he says he is and that he cares about us.
- Faith in God must be based on belief in truth, not what we see around us.
- Faith in God comes through the message of his Word.
- Faith is what pleases God.
- Without faith we are reduced to people-pleasing, approval-seeking people.
- Without faith it is impossible to live the life we were created for.
- Without faith we remain enslaved to what we can see, feel, and touch.
- Without faith we can never fully please God, even though we might win people over and please them.
- Faith is what the ancient saints were commended for.

All these people were still living by faith when they died. They did not receive the things promised; they only saw them and welcomed them from a distance. And they admitted that they were aliens and strangers on earth. People who say such things show that they are looking for a country of their own. If they had been thinking of the country they had left, they would have had opportunity to return. Instead, they were longing for a better country—a heavenly one. Therefore God is not ashamed to be called their God, for he has prepared a city for them.

Hebrews 11:13–16

What is God saying to you about faith?

2

Faith Tests

The Purpose and the Promise in the Testing of Our Faith

Life is one test after another. God wants to remove any doubt and strengthen our faith to make it pure.

Dr. Bruce Wilkinson[1]

Several years ago my friend Eileen purchased the teaching series by Dr. Bruce Wilkinson called The Testing of Your Faith. She spent the summer taking the women in leadership at our church through the series. The things Bruce taught and the insights Eileen added made that summer one of the most life-changing times of my life. Since then I have not looked at faith or tests and trials the same. I think it's important for us to look at what God says about faith and why our faith must be tested to become mature.

Count it all joy when you fall into various trials, knowing that the testing of your faith produces patience. But let patience have its perfect work, that you may be perfect and complete, lacking nothing.

James 1:2–4 NKJV

Consider it a sheer gift, friends, when tests and challenges come at you from all sides. You know that under pressure, your faith-life is forced into the open and shows its true colors. So don't try to get out of anything prematurely. Let it do its work so you become mature and well-developed, not deficient in any way.

James 1:2–4 Message

Consider it wholly joyful, my brethren, whenever you are enveloped in or encounter trials of any sort or fall into various temptations. Be assured and understand that the trial and proving of your faith bring out endurance and steadfastness and patience. But let endurance and steadfastness and patience have full play and do a thorough work, so that you may be people perfectly and fully developed with no defects, lacking in nothing.

James 1:2–4 AMP

Are you getting the picture that a life of faith in God is quite different from the way we might plan things? Scripture tells us that trials and hardships are gifts and should be looked upon with joy. In my own human understanding this sounds insane! Why would I want to open up a gift that would bring me pain of any kind?

Back to the questions. Do you want to live your best life? Do you want to live a rich, full, overflowing life? If you answered yes, there is good news and bad news. The good news is that Jesus came and died so that you can have access to abundance of life in him. He came to give you—yes, gift you—a full life. But the flip side of that, or the bad news, is that this full life, a life lacking no good thing, comes as our faith is tested, proved, tried, and made mature. There is no way around it.

During the thirty-day faith dare you will be challenged. You will be presented with a portion of biblical truth, and you will be dared to look for ways to live it out in your personal life that day. In other words you will be practicing faith one day at a time. If you think for a moment that it will come naturally or be easy, think again. You will undoubtedly be tested on what you are endeavoring to believe, live, and turn into faith habits in your life.

When something difficult comes at you, realize that your faith is being tested.

> In this you greatly rejoice, though now for a little while, if need be, you have been grieved by various trials, that the genuineness of your faith, being much more precious than gold that perishes, though it is tested by fire, may be found to praise, honor, and glory at the revelation of Jesus Christ.
>
> 1 Peter 1:6–7 NKJV

- Trials are tests of what you believe.
- You are to rejoice in the fire of the trial.
- You are to believe that testing and trials are part of God's development process.
- You are to believe that God knows about the test or trial.
- You are to believe that God is with you in the test or trial.
- You are to believe that God has the power to change you through the test or trial.
- You are to believe that since God is good, all his dealing with you is good—even tests and trials.

Our lives are about a much bigger picture than we can see. God is the creator of the bigger picture, and he is always working in his power to accomplish his plan.

In him we were also chosen, having been predestined according to the plan of him who works out everything in conformity with the purpose of his will.

Ephesians 1:11

- You have been chosen.
- You have been predestined.
- You are living a life according to the will and plan of God.
- He is working out things in your life to conform to his plan.

In this verse "works out" is taken from the Greek *energeo*, which means to be at work in or to produce.

The testing of your faith *produces something*.

Trials are tests, and though they are hard, they are good because they *produce something in us*.

To understand God and his ways, we need to see in Scripture that God is a God who is always working out everything to conform to his plan and will. Wow! Can you see how truth and understanding who God is can uplift you and encourage you in the midst of real hardships?

God is producing in you everything in conformity to the purpose of his will. Period. Now to believe this—is faith! You cannot see the outcome or the good being produced at first, but you must believe. This belief in God's development plan in your life is faith that is pleasing to God.

Count It All Joy?

If we could train our spiritual senses to look at life through God's perspective, we would understand that we have to sacrifice something to get something. When we learn to bring ourselves into the light of faith in every test and challenge, we will be able to count difficult times as a joy or a gift because we understand that these times will pass and that these times will produce good—God's intended good in us.

Every test and trial raises two important questions: What do you believe about God? How strongly do you believe it? In our trials our belief in God can override our feelings if we learn to focus on God and his track record of faithfulness rather than on our feelings of hopelessness in the current situation. If you haven't yet had a lot of personal experience with God's faithfulness, read stories of God's faithfulness to his people in Scripture.

Hard times humble us. This humbling tests what we really believe. When we endure, testing causes our faith to grow stronger and more mature. Strong and maturing faith fills us up to the fullest measure of joy—as our lives are not as dependent on feelings, people, or circumstances. We begin to transcend this world with a newfound faith in a God who is above all things.

> Be careful to follow every command I am giving you today, so that you may live and increase and may enter and possess the land that the LORD promised on oath to your forefathers. Remember how the LORD your God led you all the way in the desert these forty years, to humble you and to test you in order to know what was in your heart, whether or not you would keep his commands. He humbled you, causing you to hunger and then feeding you with manna, which neither you nor your fathers had known, to teach you that man does not live on bread alone but on every word that comes from the mouth of the LORD. Your clothes did not wear out and your feet did not swell during these forty years. Know then in your heart that as a man disciplines his son, so the LORD your God disciplines you.
>
> Deuteronomy 8:1–5

Endure hardship as discipline; God is treating you as sons. For what son is not disciplined by his father? If you are not disciplined (and everyone undergoes discipline) then you are illegitimate children and not true sons. Moreover, we have all had human fathers who disciplined us and we respected them for it. How much more should we submit to the Father of our spirits and live! Our fathers disciplined us for a little while as they thought best; but God disciplines us for our good, that we may share in his holiness. No discipline seems pleasant at the time, but painful. Later on, however, it produces a harvest of righteousness and peace for those who have been trained by it.

Hebrews 12:7–11

The testing of our faith trains us to live. This training produces peace and righteousness, which means, literally, *what is right*.

A few months back our family got a new puppy. Lucy is a mix of bichon and poodle and is adorable. Her face makes me smile because she always looks like she is smiling at me. We welcomed her into our family and love her dearly. However, she has been difficult to train. She likes to eliminate wherever she wants to. Sometimes she goes outside, but if she doesn't feel like it, she just goes wherever her little fluffy bottom feels like going. Naturally we are not happy with this behavior.

Because I love her, I am trying everything I can to train her so that she can finally understand. Today she is tethered to me on a short leash. As I write at the computer, she does not have the freedom of the house. She doesn't like this very much. I guess you could say this is her test and she is not happy. But why is she being tested? Because I love her and want what's best for her. Yes, it's painful, but there is a goal in mind.

The same is true for us. Do you ever feel like God has you on a short leash? Count it all joy—the Father is producing something in you, training you to walk with him.

Learning the Faith Walk

It all started with a few freak accidents. I blew out my calf muscle and ended up in a wheelchair for months. Then the next year I tore a tendon in my other ankle, had surgery, and landed in a wheelchair again. As a result, I needed to learn how to walk all over again. The therapy for this is called gait training, and the goal is to get the patient back to his or her normal gait. I learned a lot about the need to walk properly to prevent further injury. At first it felt awkward, but with practice it became the new normal. The same is true for learning to walk—or relearning to walk—in faith.

We practice walking and living in faith whenever we are tested or face hardship. We also practice the faith life when we make choices that are contrary to self and our own commonsense approach to things. Oswald Chambers speaks about this in *My Utmost for His Highest*:

> Can you trust Jesus Christ where your common sense cannot trust Him? Can you venture heroically on Jesus Christ's statements when the facts of your common-sense life shout—"It's a lie?" Let me say I believe God will supply all my need, and then let me run dry, with no outlook, and see whether I will go through the trial of faith, or whether I will sink back to something lower. Faith must be tested, because it can be turned into a personal possession only through conflict. What is your faith up against just now? The test will either prove that your faith is right, or it will kill it. Believe steadfastly on Him and all you come up against will develop your faith. Faith is unutterable trust in God, trust which never dreams that He will not stand by us.[2]

God Wants Us to Pass the Tests!

God has designed for us to pass the tests that he allows to come our way. He wants us to succeed. But most of us think God allows hardship so he can zap us and hurt us. This thinking, though natural, is not biblical. We need to remember what God's Word says about his love, life tests, discipline, endurance, and being conformed to his image. When we see the character of God always rooting for us, shaping us as seems best, we can applaud tests, though hard, and actually rejoice in them. How we respond to life and tests will determine the outcome. As your faith grows stronger, you become more faithful. To be faithful is actually being more filled with faith!

When we lack faith, we forget that God is involved in each of our circumstances. When we don't believe he is involved, we have trouble remembering that things will work out. We begin to compromise our faith and stop believing that God is in control. Next we begin to complain verbally about our circumstances. We move on to blame people. And in time we realize that God must be in this and we become angry with him. As we continue on the path of unbelief, we begin to tear down other people's faith.

Have you ever known someone who is passive-aggressive? They are angry, but they suppress the anger and it comes out in a passive sort of way—like withdrawing from you or giving you the silent treatment. We often act like God is passive-aggressive. We act like he's secretly angry with us and out to punish us and ruin our lives, which contradicts what he's told us in his Word. If we buy into this thinking, we might even think he is ignoring us rather than loving us. Let's face it, in times of trial it is easy to feel like God is giving us the silent treatment. But God is not passive-aggressive. He is active and always working. His love never changes. Every hardship is to test what we believe and bring us into a stronger faith relationship with God. Every hardship is an opportunity.

How Do I Live a Faith Walk When in a Test?

Sue's boyfriend of five years dumped her. Her hurt was unbearable, and she couldn't eat or sleep for days. Sue, a Christian, was so distraught that she was tempted to feel her life was over. The life she had with Chad was over, but her life in Christ was not over. This painful breakup tested everything she had professed to believe in the good times. She claimed to believe God had a plan for her life, loved her, and was directing her days. But could she believe in this same God in the bad times?

This trial tested her faith. God planned for her to pass the test and come out stronger in the end. When we are in similar situations, we too are being tested concerning what we really believe about God. Do we believe God is God? Do we believe God is sovereign and powerful? Do we believe God uses difficult circumstances to shape and mold us?

First and foremost we must believe God exists and cares enough to respond to us. Second, we must align our belief with Scripture, which says that God is aware of each test and trial and will use each one for his glory and our good. Here are some faith steps for life tests:

1. Acknowledge that this "thing" is a test—testing what you believe, not how you behave. This test was ordained just for you by the God who knows what you need.
2. An emotional response is natural and not a sin. Testing causes us to feel grieved, angry, frustrated, discouraged, or impatient. When you have a negative emotion, it is because you don't believe the truth about God. You must pay attention to these feelings, figure out what you don't believe, and ask God to help your unbelief.
3. Rather than act on emotion, stop and ask yourself the truth about the situation. Realize that you can be okay in a grievous situation when you understand that God has a purpose in it.
4. The situation does not have to change for you to find peace, but your reaction to it changes when you have faith.
5. If you continue to focus on the circumstances that upset you instead of on God, you will never have peace or contentment and will forever try to manipulate the circumstances so as to escape the test. If you do this, God will just keep bringing

you back to the test so that you can learn whatever he needs to teach you.

Faith Focus

I have been wearing contact lenses for years, and recently, I was in such a hurry that I popped in only one. I am corrected for mono-vision, which means one eye sees distance and the other is corrected to read up close. I was seeing just fine until I tried to look at the fine print on a cracker box. All of a sudden I could not see a thing. I was confused. I had my contacts in, didn't I? Yes, I did, but only one.

My eyes focused beautifully on the distance but were not able to focus on the details of the closer images. In the same way faith has much to do with focus. We are often good at having faith about far-off things but terrible at having faith in the details, in our everyday lives.

Focus is part of the faith dare. Each day you will be asked to put a magnifying lens on truth and dare yourself to walk differently because of what you see in God's Word. Focus, focus, focus.

> You will keep in perfect peace
> > him whose mind is steadfast,
> > because he trusts in you.
> Trust in the LORD forever,
> > for the LORD, the LORD, is the Rock eternal.
>
> Isaiah 26:3–4

The goal of this book is to help us develop the habit of looking at life the way the Bible shows us. This point of view brings peace and contentment, even in difficult circumstances. Most people, like the children of Israel in the wilderness, miss the fingerprints of God in their lives. Some people fail the same faith test year after year. You and I cannot generate faith for very long through human determination. Determination does not equal faith. Determination is a by-product of faith; it doesn't cause faith. God gives us his Word and his promises to use as gifts. Take them and let them make a difference in your life.

The thirty devotionals that follow offer the opportunity to set apart time to focus on God and his Word—one truth a day. Don't just read the daily selection; challenge yourself with what it says to you. Process it, digest it, memorize it, use it, breathe it in, walk it out. Live strong. Live in faith. Embrace the Spirit life within you. Every day offers a gift of growth. If we submit to the Father, we will live the richest, fullest life imaginable.

What is God speaking to you about the tests of faith and the walk of faith?

PART 2

Live Up! In Relationship to God

So if you're serious about living this new resurrection life with Christ, act like it. Pursue the things over which Christ presides. Don't shuffle along, eyes to the ground, absorbed with the things right in front of you. Look up, and be alert to what is going on around Christ—that's where the action is. See things from his perspective.

Your old life is dead. Your new life, which is your real life—even though invisible to spectators—is with Christ in God. He is your life. . . . That means killing off everything connected with that way of death. . . . That's a life shaped by things and feelings instead of by God. . . . You're done with that old life. . . .

Let every detail in your lives—words, actions, whatever—be done in the name of the Master, Jesus, thanking God the Father every step of the way.

Colossians 3:1–3, 5, 7, 17 Message

Our lives are touched by relationships with others. We live in a world filled with people and responsibilities. And yet lost in the hustle and bustle of our everyday schedules is one particular relationship that has the ability to change all the others. The relationship we often leave untended is the most important one: our relationship with God.

The Samaritan woman was like us. She had a past that she hoped could be changed into a better future. She put up with life, with disappointing relationships and the circumstances of the day. She was a sinner and she knew it. It's not that she was proud of it, but it was her life. But her view was changed the day she met a Jewish man at the watering hole, a man who promised her that if she drank the water he gave her, she would never thirst again. She hoped it could be true, and maybe you hope it could be true too.

It is time to drink from God, live our lives differently, look up into his eyes, listen closely to his voice, and find the source that will fill us in such a way that we will never thirst again. Today is the day to begin.

Day 1

The Miracle of a New Heart

Dare to Ask God for a New Heart

> As water reflects a face,
> so a man's heart reflects the man.
>
> Proverbs 27:19

Many women know the pain of a broken heart or a wounded heart, because both are part of life. But have you ever stopped to think that God wants to give you a whole and healthy heart? It's true. God's desire is to purify our hearts, cleanse our hearts, and make us completely and wholly his. Since the heart is the center of who we are, the heart will always be the focus from God's side of things.

All of life ebbs and flows from this center core of the heart. If our heart is divided in loyalty, we will move in two directions. There will be a push and a pull to our lives, creating conflict and restricting us from living in the freedom that is ours as Christ followers. Throughout Scripture we read of the importance of our heart condition and its centrality to everything concerning us. As we try to walk down two opposing paths—bitterness and blessing, the human side of us and the spiritual side of us—we will become increasingly unstable as time goes by. Rather than living a full life, we will settle for an empty life and get into the groove of living for two masters: God and self. Instead of being alive with the light and life of Christ, we will be cold and dead to the things of God. There is a better way.

God has a gift for you. You can't buy it at a trendy boutique or an exclusive department store. It is more beautifying than any spa treatment or plastic surgery. And though it's free, it is the most valuable gift you will ever receive. It's a new heart. That's right, a new center core to your entire being, changing the way you think, respond, and live. This new heart beats to the rhythm of God's heartbeat and moves to the sound of his voice. This new heart longs to stay focused and centered on the source of its life: God himself.

■ Today's Praise/Prayer: Psalm 86

> Teach me your way, O LORD,
>   and I will walk in your truth;
> give me an undivided heart,
>   that I may fear your name.
> I will praise you, O LORD my God, with all my heart;
>   I will glorify your name forever.
> For great is your love toward me,
>   you have delivered my soul from the depths of the grave.
>   . . .
> You, O LORD, are a compassionate and gracious God,
>   slow to anger, abounding in love and faithfulness.
> Turn to me and have mercy on me;
>   grant your strength to your servant.

vv. 11–13, 15–16

■ Today's Truth: Ezekiel 36:26–28; Hebrews 4:12

I will give you a new heart and put a new spirit in you; I will remove from you your heart of stone and give you a heart of flesh. I will put

46

my Spirit in you and move you to follow my decrees and be careful to keep my laws. You will live in the land I gave your forefathers; you will be my people, and I will be your God.

Ezekiel 36:26–28

I'll pour pure water over you and scrub you clean. I'll give you a new heart, put a new spirit in you. I'll remove the stone heart from your body and replace it with a heart that's God-willed, not self-willed. I'll put my Spirit in you and make it possible for you to do what I tell you and live by my commands. You'll once again live in the land I gave your ancestors. You'll be my people! I'll be your God!

Ezekiel 36:26–28 Message

For the word of God is living and active. Sharper than any double-edged sword, it penetrates even to dividing soul and spirit, joints and marrow; it judges the thoughts and attitudes of the heart.

Hebrews 4:12

This new heart is kept in proper rhythm by the truth found in God's Word and by daily surrender of self to the Father. God's Word, like a surgical instrument, goes deep within the heart, cutting away the sin and all that displeases God. Daily surrender is the path to following Jesus. We become someone different as we follow. Coming to him daily and moving in a new direction are necessary to live a life of faith. At the heart of this thirty-day dare is nothing less than your heart.

Think of the difference between the two kinds of hearts Ezekiel describes:

- heart of stone: hard, heavy, dull, cold, dead
- heart of flesh: soft, light, beating to a proper rhythm, warm, alive

or

- self-willed: wanting to do what I want, when I want to do it; having to have my own way
- God-willed: living for the purposes of God the Father

Living with a new heart does not come automatically or naturally. When someone undergoes heart transplant surgery, that person is sent home with antirejection drugs. In the same way, our natural self will want to reject the new heart God has put within us. We will want to do things the old way. But we can learn to live with the beauty and health of a new spiritual heart as an intentional part of our spiritual journey. For faith to be genuine our heart must be centered, focused, and intentionally loyal to God. We must ask God to teach us to walk in his ways. We must ask God to put us together, heart and mind—undivided. When our focus is on God, we have a healthy fear and reverence of his power and a desire to obey him.

> Give me an undivided heart,
> that I may fear your name.
>
> Psalm 86:11

Divided is defined as:

- to separate or become separated into parts (broken, frag-mented, lost from the other half)
- to separate into opposing factions (two loyalties)
- to cause to cut or to be cut off (no longer receiving from God's power source)

An undivided or centered heart is a heart that is whole, not blocked or cut off from spiritual things, and not compartmentalized into a million little places. If we want total life change, we have to be willing to let go of the areas in our heart that are blocked from God. This heart cleaning is an important step in surrendering all of ourselves to his will. It is his desire to heal us by giving us a new heart—a heart that can give love, receive love, and respond to God. A new heart—alive and beating with the heartbeat of God—centers us and brings freedom.

Beth Moore says, "We would rather God just fix our messes. We don't want to get into the reasons why. But God wants us to know why we continue being oppressed, so that the next time we're in the same situation, we'll make different choices."[1] Sometimes we don't want to see the things God is showing us about ourselves. Our inner insecurity puts up walls of protection. Admitting that we are wrong, divided, uncensored, or falling short does not feel good. Often we even bargain with God.

Unless we allow God to cut us open, search the deep things of our heart, try us, know our thoughts, and then change us from the inside out, we will stay the same. This movement toward surrendering our heart to God is intentional—done on purpose and with an aim in mind.

■ Today's Dare: Ask God for a New Heart

- Ask God to show you the areas in your heart that need healing.
- Look for the signs of fragmented parts of your heart that need to be recentered.
- Pray from Psalm 86: "Teach me your way. Give me an undivided heart."
- Thank God for the gift of a new heart. Remind yourself over and over that God has given you a gift that is a miracle—a gift money cannot buy, a gift that will never go out of style or get old—a new spiritual heart.
- Ask God to move you today to be closer to him and to follow in his ways.
- Ask God to make you a woman with one focus, one vision, one purpose.

- Dare to see yourself with a new heart today. Go back to the truth of God's promise throughout the day and thank him for your new heart. Determine to live out of that new heart from this point forward.

Journal

Acknowledging where we are is the first step to living in faith and truth.

Today's truth is speaking to me . . .

_____
_____
_____
_____
_____
_____

God is asking me to . . .

_____
_____
_____
_____
_____
_____

My challenge is to . . .

_____
_____
_____
_____
_____

■ Today's Prayer

Lord, I want to know you in ways I have never known you before. I come to you with my heart, the center of who I am. I ask you to work within me by exposing the areas that keep me divided, fragmented, and out of focus. Teach me your way and I will walk in your truth. Above all else give me an undivided heart, that I may fear your name and worship you with full and passionate surrender. Let surrender become the whole of who I am and the center desire of my heart.

For the eyes of the LORD run to and fro throughout the whole earth, to show Himself strong on behalf of those whose heart is loyal to Him.

2 Chronicles 16:9 NKJV

■ Today I Believe . . .

God promises to show himself strong on my behalf.

Day 2

Follow the Leader

■ *Dare to Pay Attention to God's Lead* ■

Whoever follows me will never walk
in darkness, but will have the
light of life.

John 8:12

I wake up to the alarm clock and begin each day. With my to-do list
in front of me it is easy to ignore anything that's not on my list.

Each day is a ministry opportunity, a chance to do all that God
has called us to do for that twenty-four-hour period. Sure, it might
be making meals, cleaning rooms, or changing diapers. Or it might
be sitting in meetings, entering computer data, or answering phones.
But no matter what is in front of us, there is a deeper purpose to
the day: to follow after Christ and pay attention to how he wants
us to live in the mundane moments of real life.

Before they became his disciples, the men who followed Jesus were
just average guys. They were minding their own business, fishing
as usual. On an ordinary workday Jesus called them into an extra–
ordinary life. This life would not come naturally to them—fishing
for fish they knew how to do, but fishing for souls? Certainly out

52

of their comfort zone. But they put down their nets, left everything behind, and went a different direction that day. Thus began the spiritual journey of the first Christ followers, our examples today.

It's easy to do the things that come naturally to us. But it's not so easy to lay down our will and follow God into the areas that are difficult or unnatural to our reasoning, feelings, or habitual ways of living. I am so glad that Jesus understands this. In fact, the disciples needed a good bit of coaching too.

It wasn't enough for the disciples to turn and follow; they had to learn to listen and obey Jesus's direction. When he asked them to lay down their nets and follow him, they were living life their way, and Jesus came to change that. He began teaching them a new way to live, and it was all about obedience. Obedience is difficult for many of us because rebellion or self-dependence is our natural way to live. I bet it wasn't much different for the disciples. They tried reasoning with the Lord. They even questioned his directives. But once they questioned and Jesus answered, they listened. Their listening ears inspired obedient hearts. We could learn a lot from them about listening and obeying.

Today's Praise/Prayer: Psalm 119

Happy are all who perfectly follow the laws of God. Happy are all who search for God, and always do his will, rejecting compromise with evil, and walking only in his paths. You have given us your laws to obey—oh how I want to follow them consistently. Then I will not be disgraced, for I will have a clean record.

After you have corrected me I will thank you by living as I should! I *will* obey!

vv. 1–8

Today's Truth: Mark 1:16–18; Luke 5:4–7

As Jesus walked beside the Sea of Galilee, he saw Simon and his brother Andrew casting a net into the lake, for they were fishermen. "Come, follow me," Jesus said, "and I will make you fishers of men." At once they left their nets and followed him.

Mark 1:16–18

When he had finished speaking, he said to Simon, "Put out into deep water, and let down the nets for a catch."

Simon answered, "Master, we've worked hard all night and haven't caught anything. But because you say so, I will let down the nets."

When they had done so, they caught such a large number of fish that their nets began to break. So they signaled to their partners in the other boat to come and help them, and they came and filled both boats so full that they began to sink.

Luke 5:4–7

In the passage from Mark, the disciples had to do two things to fulfill God's call:

1. come: to approach, to advance toward, to exist in a particular place or point
2. follow: to pursue, to go after, to accompany, to comply with and obey, to pay attention to

We too must do those two things!

Jesus called the disciples to come. He required that they follow. He promised an outcome—he would make them something different! They didn't look different. They were still human flesh people. But their outcome was different. Their lives were different because of Jesus. They were not just about the temporal anymore—catching fish for food. They were about the Father's business with an eternal focus—catching souls for eternity.

The passage in Luke takes place at the Lake of Gennesaret. Jesus was teaching from one of the fishing boats, and when he finished speaking he told Peter to let down the nets for a catch. It didn't make any logical sense. Peter had fished all night with no results, and now Jesus was telling him to let down his nets. But we see pure and simple obedience recorded here. Though Simon questioned, the bottom line was that he obeyed.

I love Peter's words, "But because you say so, I will . . ."

What about us? Many times we get great ideas and dreams and run with them. We run and run, plan and plan, until we run out of steam. We burn out. But there is a better way. What if we made it a daily practice to come and follow? What would that look like? How could that change our life?

To come and follow is a daily call of surrender to the God who made us. When we do this, we approach him each new day and move toward him in fresh relationship. Coming to Christ daily is a directional shift and means making the choice to walk with Jesus that particular day. Coming to him is the first step; following is the next step.

Following takes the choice of coming a step further. When we follow, we chase after God and his dreams for us. We comply with his voice, obey his lead, and, most importantly, we pay attention to him!

How do we pay attention to God? We make time to listen. We read his Word and pay attention to what it is saying to us personally. Each day we make it a habit to ask for the grace to make the choice to obey his Word—the grace to come and follow. We then begin moving in the direction of God's leading step by step.

What changes? He makes us different. He gives us a new heart and then calls us to follow after his ways. That is the wonder of the miracle of Christ in our midst. He is a life changer, a people mover, a restorer of all things. Some call him the difference maker. This difference at work in us is the work of regeneration and restoration. Jesus changes lives. Period. He doesn't do it by force. We have a choice each day; we have to come and follow. He is the miracle worker, but we must daily come.

Where are you today? Have you learned to be a good follower, or are you trying to take the lead in your life? This may sound simplistic, but if you are repeating the same cycle over and over, stop the insanity and ask yourself these questions: Are you coming to Jesus daily and learning to follow his work in your life? Are you listening and taking God's Word seriously? Are you in his Word more than just on Sunday morning? Are you trying to take the lead and expecting a blessing to follow you? Or are you laying down your own dreams, as well as negative habits, and asking God to change you as you follow him? Only you can make the choice that will lead to life change, and only Christ can make the lasting difference.

Today's Dare: Pay Attention to God's Lead

- What is God telling you to do today?
- What are you doubting or questioning about this directive?
- According to Scripture, what would happen if you would just obey, because he said to do something?
- Make time for listening today. Go to a place where you can be alone. It can be a locked bathroom, a parked car, beside a field—whatever. Just find a place. While in that place, for ten minutes think about what it would mean to follow God rather than self. Think of things that might change. Do you want to experience God in this life? You can. It happens when you listen and obey. Commit to God whatever first came to your mind as you listened to him.
- Dare to do the very thing God first spoke to you, the thing in front of you that you have probably put off.
- Dare to see all things today as spiritual in nature, even though they are physical, practical acts.

Journal

Acknowledging where we are is the first step to living in faith and truth.

Today's truth is speaking to me . . .

_____
_____
_____
_____
_____
_____
_____

God is asking me to . . .

_____
_____
_____
_____
_____
_____

My challenge is to . . .

_____
_____
_____
_____
_____

■ Today's Prayer

Father, so often I don't understand what you are leading me to do. Your principles can seem outdated, and I am tempted to think that my way is the best way. I bet that is how Simon felt. You told him to do something that seemed silly. It was a test, and you showed him yourself in a giant measure! I want to experience you in a giant measure. I want to do

*something just because you said so. I want to lay
down my net. Help me follow you this way.*

If anyone loves me, he will obey my teaching.

John 14:23

■ Today I Believe . . .

I love you, Lord. I will follow you and your Word.

Day 3

Living Loved

Dare to Live Differently by Living Like You Are Loved

I have loved you with an everlasting
love;
I have drawn you with loving-
kindness.
I will build you up again
and you will be rebuilt.

Jeremiah 31:3–4

"Debbie, I have never loved you." Those words, spoken to me by my husband of thirteen years, ripped out my heart and confirmed a negative belief I had carried around my entire life—that I was unloveable. Maybe for other reasons you can relate. Or maybe you have always felt loved, but you are living life loved by people but not in the reality of God's love.

I have not always lived loved—by people or in conscious acknowledgment of God's love. Truth is, I have lived insecure, fearful,

59

and with a chronic belief that I would never be enough. This belief system began forming from the time I was very young. Affected by the messages of childhood and the hurts of the past, I saw myself in a way that was not God's view of me at all.

My reality was that I was a "not-enough girl," and this little girl followed me right into adulthood, where I learned to cover up the fear and insecurity with the right words, the right look, the right deeds. In an attempt to realize love, I moved further and further away from the love of God for me and deeper into the pit of self-focus, self-preservation, and self-centeredness. Jesus always had something more—this was not his best life for me. My Good Shepherd wanted to lead me into green pastures of soul rest, identity security, and unconditional love.

Today's Praise/Prayer: Psalm 136

> Give thanks to the LORD, for he is good.
>> His love endures forever.
> Give thanks to the God of gods.
>> His love endures forever.
> Give thanks to the Lord of lords:
>> His love endures forever.
> to him who alone does great wonders,
>> His love endures forever.
> who by his understanding made the heavens,
>> His love endures forever. . . .
> to the One who remembered us in our low estate
>> His love endures forever.
> and freed us from our enemies,
>> His love endures forever.
> and who gives food to every creature.
>> His love endures forever.
> Give thanks to the God of heaven.
>> His love endures forever.

vv. 1–5, 23–26

■ Today's Truth: Romans 5:8; 1 John 3:1; 4:16; Jude 21

But God demonstrates his own love for us in this: While we were still sinners, Christ died for us.

Romans 5:8

How great is the love the Father has lavished on us, that we should be called children of God! And that is what we are!

1 John 3:1

And so we know and rely on the love God has for us. God is love.

1 John 4:16

Keep yourselves in God's love as you wait for the mercy of our Lord Jesus Christ to bring you to eternal life.

Jude 21

When it comes to following Christ, we do so by following the melody of his love for us. He led the disciples because he loved them, ultimately loving them all the way to the cross. They were people like us, doing their own thing when he called them to follow. He loved them, sinners though they were, as people for whom his life and love would make a difference.

We need to pour God's love into our learning center—our mind— so it can make its way into our hearts. It is not natural to live feeling loved by God, because we cannot see or touch him. We learn to live loved by taking his Word of truth by faith. In doing so he replaces our fears with a wonderful peace that some of us have heard about but have never experienced firsthand. I had been a Christian for many years before I began to experience the reality of God's love for me. It changed everything and continues to do so each day.

John says that God has lavished his love on us. *Lavished*, according to the dictionary, is a profuse or extravagant display of something. In the thesaurus *lavish* is linked to the word *shower*.

God showers us with his love. This extravagant covering, when realized by faith, can calm us, center us, and build confidence in us.

A child needs a parent's care, protection, love, and direction. This is what God wants to provide for each of us. As simple as it sounds, we are his children. How many of us live as daughters of God? I think we need to challenge ourselves not to overlook this basic yet profound truth. It is the foundation on which healthy relationships with God and others are built.

When we live as one who is loved, we live differently. Life is no longer a set of unfortunate circumstances but instead a journey with the Father. When we live as one who is loved, we have a changed viewpoint. Our focus is the bigger picture of God's unseen plan. When we live as one who is loved, we can walk in faith, believing in something we cannot see but dare to hope for. This faith pleases God. Are you living as one who is loved today? Or are you still defined by the labels and mistakes of your past?

■ Today's Dare: Live Like You Are Loved

- Today live up to what God calls you—his child!
- Today walk that truth as you interact with others—because they are his children too.
- Think of what it means to be a child—dependent, trusting, longing for acceptance. Remember that without faith it is impossible to please your heavenly Father. Ask God to help you in any area of unbelief regarding your true identity as his.
- Today dare yourself to do one of the following (or more if you would like):
  1. Set a timer on your phone, computer, or watch for every hour or every few hours. When it goes off, praise God for his love and ask him to make it real to you. Remind yourself of the truth that God lavishes his love on you.

2. Make a list of the "other" things you have been called—labels and names that are negative and not in alignment with the truth. Give them to God one by one. Then take a black marker and blot those labels off your list!

3. Think of the things you readily call other people. Are they contrary to how God views them? Challenge yourself to change your thinking about yourself and others as well.

4. Find something you can do to lavish love on another person in a practical way (a special meal, an errand run, a kind word, a gift, etc.).

Journal

Acknowledging where we are is the first step to living in faith and truth.

Today's truth is speaking to me . . .

_____

_____

_____

_____

_____

_____

God is asking me to . . .

_____

_____

_____

_____

_____

_____

_____

My challenge is to . . .

_____

_____

_____

_____

_____

■ Today's Prayer

> *Lord, I often feel alone. Many days I am stuck in a rut of shame or insecurity. In these places that pull me down to the world's level of thinking, I forget your love for me. Thank you that your love is profuse, extravagant, and overflowing. In a world filled with people, you care enough to lavish your love on me—because you call me your own child. That is who I am. I desire to treat others the way you treat me. I desire to live loved and to live in your love in my relationships.*

If God is for us, who can be against us?

Romans 8:31

■ Today I Believe . . .

I am God's child, and he is for me.

Day 4

Dedicated to Living as His

Dare to Live Like You Belong to God

> "For in him we live and move and
> have our being." As some of your
> own poets have said, "We are his
> offspring."
>
> Acts 17:28

He was four years old—a darling towheaded preschooler who completely stole my heart. My first child, my heartbeat, my life, my daily trial and joy! So it may come as no surprise that when he asked to belong to Jesus while we were grocery shopping one day, I was delighted. He had been to a vacation Bible school, where he had heard about becoming a part of God's family. Insistent on not waiting a moment longer, he pulled at my shorts and said, "Mommy, I want to be a part of God's family." Melted, I snatched him up into my arms, sat him in the seat of the shopping cart, and led him in a pint-sized salvation prayer right then and there. Routine grocery shopping became a sacred experience on that sunny July day.

Now that little boy is an adult. He has gone through valleys, broken places, and disappointment. But he was forever changed that day in the bakery aisle! And he has spent years growing into that change, experiencing the power of that change, and learning to live by the power and voice of the change maker—Jesus Christ.

When we come to Christ, something happens in us—something beautiful, something powerful, and something that marks us as one no longer belonging to ourselves or this world.

Today's Praise/Prayer: Psalm 100

> Shout for joy to the LORD, all the earth.
>> Serve the LORD with gladness;
>> come before him with joyful songs.
> Know that the LORD is God.
>> It is he who made us, and we are his;
>> we are his people, the sheep of his pasture.

vv. 1–3

Today's Truth: 1 Corinthians 6:19–20; 2 Corinthians 5:14–15; Ephesians 1:5, 7, 13–14; Colossians 1:27

Do you not know that your body is a temple of the Holy Spirit, who is in you, whom you have received from God? You are not your own; you were bought at a price. Therefore honor God with your body.

1 Corinthians 6:19–20

For Christ's love compels us, because we are convinced that one died for all, and therefore all died. And he died for all, that those who live should no longer live for themselves but for him who died for them and was raised again.

2 Corinthians 5:14–15

In love he predestined us to be adopted as his sons through Jesus Christ. . . . In him we have redemption through his blood. . . . Having

66

believed, you were marked in him with a seal, the promised Holy Spirit, who is a deposit guaranteeing our inheritance.

Ephesians 1:5, 7, 13–14

Christ in you, the hope of glory.

Colossians 1:27

Webster's defines *temple* as a place or house of worship, a place dedicated for a special purpose. Scripture describes our earthly bodies as temples or tents. Our body is a temple where the Holy Spirit dwells. Our life lived through this earthly vessel is a place dedicated for a special purpose. Do we live on purpose? Do we honor the truth that we are set apart as women belonging to God? If I took the temple truth seriously, would I be different?

How would I live?

How would I speak of myself?

How would I think of myself?

Would I abuse or neglect myself?

Would I stand in awe of God more often if I realized he was in me and wanted to work through me?

Everything else is secondary. God will guide us in our career choices and the other life decisions we need to make, but his primary concern isn't whether we become a dentist, hairstylist, teacher, or salesperson. The most important thing to God is that we live in the truth of who we are in him. In a society in which women are prone to look negatively at themselves and strive to find something that makes them feel valuable, this truth makes a world of difference.

Why, then, does it take so long to realize that difference?

Fireworks didn't appear in the sky the night I received Christ as my Savior. I passed from death into life, and something happened in that moment that was meant to change everything. Maybe fireworks would have gotten my attention. After an experience meant to change everything, why do we still trudge through life as if we have no hope, no help? Why do we often live as though we are no different from a nonbeliever?

Where were you when you gave your heart to Jesus? It doesn't matter if you were young or old. When you became a Christian, you became completely and totally his—body, soul, and spirit. And as his you are now a temple of the living God. There is a different life to be lived.

Today's Dare: Live Like You Belong to God

- Recognize what Scripture says about your life. You are meant to live a life set apart.
- Today live differently in response to this truth.
- Where were you when you began your journey with Jesus? Were you four or forty? Did you realize the magnitude of Christ in you? Keep that reality fresh in your mind today.
- Break down the truth of belonging to Jesus:
  - » Coming to Jesus is the first step.
  - » Following him is a lifestyle that requires denying self daily.
  - » Following requires taking up your "cross" daily.
  - » Following him each day means walking away from self and toward him.
- Ask God to make these truths real to you today:
  - » You are new.
  - » You are in Christ.
  - » You are his temple.
  - » You do not belong to yourself but to God.

» You are his ambassador, representative, and light in this dark world.

» He is working in you and desires to work through you.

• Write these truths on an index card and read them during the course of the day. Tell yourself many times today one simple word of truth: his.

■ Journal

Acknowledging where we are is the first step to living in faith and truth.

Today's truth is speaking to me . . .

_____

_____

_____

_____

_____

_____

God is asking me to . . .

_____

_____

_____

_____

_____

_____

My challenge is to . . .

_____

_____

_____

_____

_____

Today's Prayer

*Lord, life seems to be a constant back-and-forth
struggle as I grow up in you. One day up, the next
day down. Help me to stay connected to the truth
that you live in me and want me to be set apart so
that wherever I am you can do your will through me.
Take your Word, which is living and active, and plant
the truth of who I am deep in my heart. Help me
remember that I belong to you.*

We are therefore Christ's ambassadors, as though God were making
his appeal through us.

2 Corinthians 5:20

Today I Believe . . .

I am a representative of Christ in this world, and he desires to
work through me.

Day 5

Not Conformed to This World

*Dare to Believe You Are
No Longer of This World*

Jesus said, "My kingdom is not of
this world."

John 18:36

I grew up in the budding women's liberation movement. Women were liberated to do their own thing, think their own way, prove their own power, and be independent of everything that held them down. This type of independence has been with us ever since. We want to do our own thing, and with that mentality, Christians are not living different from the world. The world teaches us we can have it all, be it all, and experience it all. If being independent and liberated is so wonderful, why are we a culture of depressed and disappointed women?

Sadly, the world's way is not what it's built up to be. There are drawbacks to doing things our own way. And often buying into the "me" mentality gets us trapped in habits, relationships, and lifestyles that hurt us in the end. When life is all about us, there is not much room for God. When there isn't room for God, we live conformed to our culture, aligned to the world.

71

I started living life my way very young. Even after becoming a Christian, I still wanted to live my way with a little Jesus on top. Naturally, I didn't admit that, but that is how I lived. I experienced a wake-up call when my life fell apart during a divorce in my mid-thirties. That got my attention, and I asked God for a do-over. I wanted to make a U-turn and spend my life being conformed to his way and his Word. Such a life does not involve only what we think of as spiritual matters, but practical life as well—what we eat, how we live, how we respond to people, what we are given over to. Completely submitting to God is what faith is about.

In yet another wake-up call, I was on a gurney being transported to the cardiac care unit. No way! I was much too young. But it *was* me on the gurney being taken to a room with glass walls, monitors, and doctors who would tell me I had some arterial blockages.

It was a wake-up call on both the spiritual side and the practical side. Truth is, all of life is spiritual, and in God's eyes a line does not divide the two. But I wanted to live my way. What did eating and drinking, exercising and sleeping have to do with being spiritual? As I am learning, they have everything to do with our spiritual life. The world we live in says that all of life belongs to us, but God's Word tells us that all of life belongs to him. As his we are to conform to his ways rather than to the ways of the world. Nothing about us belongs to us! We are Christ's ambassadors. Living as his, in close relationship with him, is also living in a new reality—Christ is Lord over all parts of us. Everything about our lives is to be lived for him, who made us, redeemed us, and has a design for our life.

I often took my health for granted, but my medical wake-up call gave me an opportunity to realize, once again, that I am not of this world, because my life is in Christ. Once again, I realized I should no longer be conformed to the world's "me" philosophy.

No more my way with a little Jesus on top. No more Jesus plus everything else. To be changed, it had to be just Jesus.

Christ has given me the miracle of a new spiritual heart. He placed his Spirit within me and called me to follow him and to live as his—yes, even in this crazy world. As a born-again believer, my primary residence is not earth; I am just passing through. I am now a citizen of a different kingdom, God's kingdom.

Today we study Romans 12, but before we dive in, let's back up to the last few verses of chapter 11. Chapter 12 starts with "therefore," and we need to determine *what it is there for*!

> Oh, the depth of the riches of the wisdom and knowledge
> of God!
> How unsearchable his judgments,
> and his paths beyond tracing out!
> "Who has known the mind of the Lord?
> Or who has been his counselor?"
> "Who has ever given to God,
> that God should repay him?"
> For from him and through him and to him are all things.
> To him be the glory forever! Amen.
>
> Romans 11:33–36

▦ Today's Praise/Prayer: Psalm 51

> Have mercy on me, O God,
> according to your unfailing love;
> according to your great compassion
> blot out my transgressions.
> Wash away all my iniquity
> and cleanse me from my sin.
> For I know my transgressions,
> and my sin is always before me.
> Against you, you only, have I sinned
> and done what is evil in your sight,

so that you are proved right when you speak
and justified when you judge.
Surely I was sinful at birth,
sinful from the time my mother conceived me.
Surely you desire truth in the inner parts;
you teach me wisdom in the inmost place.
Cleanse me with hyssop, and I will be clean;
wash me, and I will be whiter than snow.
Let me hear joy and gladness;
let the bones you have crushed rejoice.
Hide your face from my sins
and blot out all my iniquity.
Create in me a pure heart, O God,
and renew a steadfast spirit within me.
Do not cast me from your presence
or take your Holy Spirit from me.
Restore to me the joy of your salvation
and grant me a willing spirit, to sustain me.

vv. 1–12

■ Today's Truth: Romans 12:1; Colossians 1:16–17

Therefore, I urge you, brothers, in view of God's mercy, to offer your bodies as living sacrifices, holy and pleasing to God—this is your spiritual act of worship.

Romans 12:1

So here's what I want you to do, God helping you: Take your everyday, ordinary life—your sleeping, eating, going-to-work, and walking-around life—and place it before God as an offering.

Romans 12:1 Message

For by him all things were created: things in heaven and on earth, visible and invisible, whether thrones or powers or rulers or authorities; all things were created by him and for him. He is before all things, and in him all things hold together.

Colossians 1:16–17

Living sacrifi...
can crawl off th...
daily, surrender...
very well. We v...
rights and stri...
God in a way...
new and fresh...
that is difficu...

You see, t...
and the end...
and lights e...
in response...
to stay cor...
us and in...
are to sta...
surrende...
any pow...
love we...
Whe...
offering our p...
their faculties. This is where it gets ......, though
we own ourselves. Once we surrender ourselves to the God who made us, loves us, and has forgiven us, God begins to do amazing things in our lives.

Why is this surrender so difficult? The spiritual journey starts with surrender, but many of us don't get past the starting gate, do we? We feel as though our bodies, our physical selves, should belong to us, and the idea of giving them over to God . . . well, seems a bit impractical. That is, until we realize that this *is* the starting point. I didn't want to change my diet, and quite frankly, I am not a fan of exercise. But if my body truly isn't my own, and heart disease is the diagnosis, it would be disrespectful to God to hold on to my own rights over it, wouldn't it? I admit I cried at every meal for a few weeks. But I will also admit that I gained a closer walk with God through this surrender of self.

Why is this physical sacrifice a spiritual act of worship? It is an intentional surrendering of our self, as we know it, to the God who made us. It is coming into agreement with his Word, which says we don't belong to ourselves anyway.

Worship? I thought worship meant singing a hymn. I thought worship was a beautifully worded prayer. Worship? Yes, according to Scripture a spiritual act of worship is surrender of our self, our *real* self, body, soul, spirit, to the God who made us. This includes how we treat our physical body, the lifestyle we choose to live, the things that we allow access to our heart, and the very practical place of our mind.

> Do you not know that your body is a temple of the Holy Spirit, who is in you, whom you have received from God? You are not your own; you were bought at a price. Therefore honor God with your body.
>
> 1 Corinthians 6:19–20

■ Today's Dare: Believe You Are No Longer of This World

- Today reflect on this thought of giving your life completely over to God as a surrender, and yes, a sacrifice.

- Examine your lifestyle choices. Do you eat healthy? Do you exercise regularly? Do you take any precaution for existing medical conditions? Do you sleep, rest, manage stress?

- What could God be saying to you about the spirituality behind presenting your body to him? Think about that today and let God speak to your heart.

- Give up all snack foods or special pleasure foods today. As you sacrifice the pleasure of grabbing a snack, let it remind you that you are to give up of your entire self to God regularly.

■ Journal

Acknowledging where we are is the first step to living in faith and truth.

Today's truth is speaking to me . . .

_____

_____

_____

_____

_____

_____

_____

God is asking me to . . .

_____

_____

_____

_____

_____

_____

_____

My challenge is to . . .

_____

_____

_____

_____

_____

■ Today's Prayer

Lord, you made me, and though I often think I am my own, I really am not. Teach me to live as one who is no longer about self but about the God who made her, for his purposes. Only then can I become my best self. Conform me to the image of your Son and your plan for my life. Show me what the sacrifice of giving myself to you looks like.

But now he has reconciled you by Christ's physical body through death to present you holy in his sight, without blemish and free from accusation—if you continue in your faith, established and firm, not moved from the hope held out in the gospel.

Colossians 1:22–23

Today I Believe . . .

I am holy in his sight. I do not belong to the world but to the God who loves me.

Day 6

Transformed Lives

░ *Dare to Renew Your Mind in God's Word* ░

Faith comes from hearing the
message, and the message is
heard through the word of Christ.

Romans 10:17

The Samaritan woman at the well was tired. She was used up and getting by. Many of us know exactly how she felt. We might feel used up by work, too many hats of responsibility to wear, or too many people to please. Life is complicated, especially when people are involved. They are human, like us, and can hurt us, disappoint us, and cause us some of the greatest pain we face.

Most of us want different lives. As Christians it's tempting to think that the difference involves merely cleaning up the outer trappings that identified us with the world before Christ. We become churchgoers instead of party girls, give part of our income to the poor instead of the bartender, and go to Bible studies instead of reading steamy romance novels. We are different, at least by all outside standards. But are we different where it counts?

Cleaning up our life is just an external fix to an internal situation. To be truly changed we must have interior work done, a work that starts at the processing station of our life: our mind.

Our mind is the control center of our life. What we think eventually becomes a belief, and we live by what we really believe, not by what we say we believe. We have learned to think like the world thinks, plan like the world plans, find value in what the world values, and act like the world acts. In other words we have learned from a young age how to conform to the standards or patterns of the world. Today we will continue with the theme of not belonging to ourselves, not being of this world, and not conforming to the pattern of this world—but being transformed by God.

■ Today's Praise/Prayer: Psalm 119

> How can a young man keep his way pure?
>   By living according to your word.
> I seek you with all my heart;
>   do not let me stray from your commands.
> I have hidden your word in my heart
>   that I might not sin against you.

vv. 9–11

■ Today's Truth: Deuteronomy 30:19–20; Joshua 24:15; Romans 12:2–3

Now choose life, so that you and your children may live and that you may love the LORD your God, listen to his voice, and hold fast to him. For the LORD is your life.

Deuteronomy 30:19–20

But if serving the LORD seems undesirable to you, then choose for yourselves this day whom you will serve.

Joshua 24:15

Do not conform any longer to the pattern of this world, but be transformed by the renewing of your mind. Then you will be able to test and approve what God's will is—his good, pleasing and perfect will. For by the grace given me I say to every one of you: Do not think of yourself more highly than you ought, but rather think of yourself with sober judgment, in accordance with the measure of faith God has given you.

Romans 12:2–3

We have the power of choice. Can you see it? God allows us the opportunity each day to choose whom we will serve, whom we will live for, which road we will travel. When we choose life and the Lord, our choice affects our children and their children. There is a lot at stake, and choosing God's way has eternal ramifications.

The words *any longer* tell us that we have already become accustomed to the way the world thinks. We are not to think this way one second longer! Do not conform *any longer*. We are not to be like this world; we are not to be cut from its pattern. We are also to have a different view of ourselves—not too little, not too much—just a biblical view.

Let's take a look at a few key words here:

- conform: to become similar in form or character; to act or be in compliance with
- pattern: a model to imitate or to use for the purpose of making things
- transformed: to change in nature, function, or condition
- renewing: to make new again or to restore

According to Scripture, I am not to become similar in character or form to the model I see in this world. Instead, God calls me to be changed from a person who is patterned after the world, society, or culture to a person who is made new and restored mentally. Why do you think this transformation has to take place first and foremost in the mind? Our minds are changed by the truth of God's Word. God's Word is living and active, having the power to set us free and change us from the inside out.

One thing is for sure: God allows U-turns, and today you may need to make a major turn in order to experience all that God has for you.

Do you think biblically about yourself? The true route to freedom and healing of a damaged self-esteem is not to pump yourself up with a makeover or a motivational seminar. Rather, let God build you up in the truth about who you are in Christ and the truth about his involvement in your life.

To think of myself with sober judgment involves taking a candid look at who I am, how I am living, and to whom I belong. It is humility of thought about myself. This humility does not make me a doormat to the world, but it does find strength in God rather than in myself. This humility is dependence. This humility involves understanding that God is my provider and looking to him in all things.

You may be thinking, isn't that a no-brainer? Don't all Christians trust in God this way?

No. It would be great if we all thought less of ourselves and more of God. It would be great if we attributed the good and the strength we see in ourselves to God. But it's not usually so. Why? Because it's natural for us to trust in ourselves.

Let's try something supernatural!

■ Today's Dare: Renew Your Mind in God's Word

- Today think on these things:

Man does not live on bread alone, but on every word that comes from the mouth of God.

Matthew 4:4

If you hold to my teaching, you are really my disciples. Then you will know the truth, and the truth will set you free.

John 8:31–32

For the word of God is living and active. Sharper than any double-edged sword, it penetrates even to dividing soul and spirit, joints and marrow; it judges the thoughts and attitudes of the heart.

Hebrews 4:12

How can a young [woman] keep [her] way pure?
By living according to your word.

Psalm 119:9

- Today ask yourself what your *real* values are. I am not talking about the spiritually correct answer but what they really are. Examine your heart and mind to determine if your values are in line with the world or if they are undivided and in sync with what God values.
- Today dare yourself to choose an action that is in line with God's ideals, that is opposite of what you desire to do.

Journal

Acknowledging where we are is the first step to living in faith and truth.

Today's truth is speaking to me . . .

_____

_____

_____

_____

_____

_____

God is asking me to . . .

_____

_____

_____

_____

_____

_____

_____

My challenge is to . . .

_____

_____

_____

_____

_____

■ Today's Prayer

> *Father, speak to me about my lifestyle. Show me where I conform to this world. Jesus, renew me, restore me, and turn me around to face you . . . face to face, heart to heart, yours and only yours.*

You were bought at a price; do not become slaves of men.

1 Corinthians 7:23

■ Today I Believe . . .

Jesus paid the price for me, so I will not live as a slave to people or this world.

Day 7

The Power of God

Dare to Believe in God's Power in All Circumstances

> For since the creation of the world
> God's invisible qualities—his
> eternal power and divine nature—
> have been clearly seen, being
> understood from what has been
> made, so that men are without
> excuse.
>
> Romans 1:20

Power is an amazing thing. Without it we would not have many of the conveniences we take for granted—things like lights and electricity, music playing from our stereo, the ability to blow-dry our hair, the joy of waking up to fresh coffee, or the ability to wash our clothes and dishes with ease. Without power we would miss out on many of the things that are a part of our everyday routine. Just experience a power outage and you will quickly realize that without power we feel lost.

Power is invisible, so we forget about it. We usually take it for granted. The same thing is often true about God's power. God's

85

power is within each of us. But do we operate in that power? Or do we rely on our own power? Our power is inferior to God's great power, but many of us live in this inferior mode. Often we take God's power for granted and fail to tap into it even though it is in us and available to us each day.

Often we mistakenly think that power is given to the people who are "really" used by God. You know, the ministers, pastors, worship leaders, and such. We fail to realize that God gives his power to all Christians, no matter what their calling in life. God's power is given to mothers, grandmothers, and students. God's power is given to missionaries, Bible teachers, and pastors. God's power is given to young girls and old ladies. God's power is given to us because of what Christ did on the cross.

Today's Praise/Prayer: Psalm 89

> You rule over the surging sea;
>> when its waves mount up, you still them. . . .
>> with your strong arm you scattered your enemies.
> The heavens are yours, and yours also the earth;
>> you founded the world and all that is in it.
> You created the north and the south; . . .
> Your arm is endued with power;
>> your hand is strong, your right hand exalted.

vv. 9–13

Today's Truth: John 15:16; 2 Corinthians 5:20; Ephesians 1:18–20; 2:10

> I chose you to go and bear fruit—fruit that will last.

John 15:16

> We are therefore Christ's ambassadors, as though God were making his appeal through us.

2 Corinthians 5:20

I pray also that the eyes of your heart may be enlightened in order that you may know the hope to which he has called you, the riches of his glorious inheritance in the saints, and his incomparably great power for us who believe. That power is like the working of his mighty strength, which he exerted in Christ when he raised him from the dead.

Ephesians 1:18–20

For we are God's workmanship, created in Christ Jesus to do good works, which God prepared in advance for us to do.

Ephesians 2:10

Paul was praying for the church in Ephesus to understand that God had called them and that they had received a glorious inheritance. He also wanted them to know that they had received great power and that this power was a working of mighty strength. Why was this his prayer? In chapter 2 he tells them that though they used to follow the ways of the world, now they are alive in Christ. Paul concludes with a verse you may know:

For we are God's workmanship, created in Christ Jesus to do good works.

Ephesians 2:10

Paul didn't just tell them, "Get to work!" He cast the vision of truth out to them, that they were different because of Christ, and that as those alive in Christ they could walk in all the good things God had prepared for them.

This is what it means to live in God's design for our lives, and doing so with the assurance of his power at work in us rather than with the flimsy notion that we can become strong enough for the task. Life gets exciting when we realize that a resurrection took place within us when we became Christ's, and now we are filled with the Holy Spirit.

- You are chosen by God.
- He has appointed you to bear fruit.
- It is his will that your fruit will come from his power, thus being lasting fruit.
- You are his ambassador.
- His plan is to make himself known in this world through your life.
- You are his work, his poem, his masterpiece.
- You have been born again and created in Christ Jesus for his work.
- He has already planned the good work he desires you to do.

God has given us his power and equipped us for a purpose. His plans for our lives fit into his bigger picture. We represent him, as ambassadors of his love, grace, and power in this world. An ambassador is a diplomat of the highest rank or a representative to another. It is exciting to think that God has called me and created me to be his representative. But as his representative, I must always keep in mind that I am not to go out under my own power and represent myself. I am to walk under authority to him in this world as his representative, his ambassador, his woman.

The first part of a building project is the foundation. Today think of the above verses and let them wash over you with God-given identity and direction so that the foundation will be newly poured in your mind. Dare to walk in the truth of being appointed by God in your everyday, average, ordinary life. We do this by listening for his gentle nudges throughout the day. Acknowledge before him that you are his and as such want to hear from him regarding today's assignment.

Today's Dare: Believe in God's Power in All Circumstances

- Today reflect several times on today's truth verses.

- Let the truth rise up within you. Pray it as a prayer of agreement: "Father, I thank you that your power is alive within me today. Use my life according to your power."
- Think of what power is and what power does in the natural realm, and then realize that God's power, which resurrected the dead, is bigger and grander than any power we can imagine. Just think . . . you are filled with that bigger and grander power because of your connection to Christ!
- Let truth fill you today and give you a purpose.
- Go into a dark room and sit in the darkness. Turn on the light and feel the difference the light makes. Remember the power of God's light and life in your life.
- Dare to take the light with you wherever you go today. Ask God how you can bless others today with the light of his love. Imagine yourself as an ambassador of love, and spread that love today.

Journal

Acknowledging where we are is the first step to living in faith and truth.

Today's truth is speaking to me . . .

_____

_____

_____

_____

_____

_____

_____

_____

_____

God is asking me to . . .

_____

_____

_____

_____

_____

My challenge is to . . .

_____

_____

_____

_____

Today's Prayer

> *Lord, I thank you that you did not leave me without you in this world. You gave me your Spirit, and you've placed your power within me. Please help me to remember that your power, mighty in strength, lives within me. Remind me to live in that power as an overcomer in the hard places of life. Let the truth of your power enable me to take faith risks each day—risking to love, to forgive, to do the right things, risking to share the gospel, to make a stand, or to change the world.*

> Blessed are those who hunger and thirst for righteousness,
> for they will be filled.
>
> Matthew 5:6

Today I Believe . . .

When I hunger for God, he is faithful to fill me up with more of Jesus and his power.

Day 8

The Power Connection

Dare to Plug into the Power Source

My grace is sufficient for you, for
my power is made perfect in
weakness.

2 Corinthians 12:9

Each day we plug something in . . . a hair dryer, a flat iron, a curling iron, a coffeemaker (though when it comes to coffee, I would prefer an IV drip!). We all know about plugging in. When I speak at retreats, I often use my hair dryer as a visual aid. I point out that the manufacturer made this particular hair dryer for a specific purpose . . . to blow hot air, to dry wet hair! But one thing has to happen before my hair dryer can operate as the manufacturer intended. It must be plugged into an electrical outlet for power. Without being plugged in, my hair dryer cannot operate as planned. The same is true for us.

Each of us was created for a specific purpose. Our manufacturer, the Almighty God, has a design for each individual life. You may not feel like you are a likely candidate for God to work through. That's the beauty of it—none of us is. We don't deserve his love, yet he loves us. We didn't deserve a break and a new life, yet he freely gave them. And we are unable to do the Christ walk in our own strength—and so he himself provides the power!

Here is the secret: what was intended for us spiritually cannot take place unless we are plugged into the outlet of all power . . . Jesus Christ. Let's take a look at what God said about this power connection.

■ Today's Praise/Prayer: Psalm 86

> Hear, O LORD, and answer me,
>> for I am poor and needy.
> Guard my life, for I am devoted to you.
>> You are my God; save your servant
>> who trusts in you.
> Have mercy on me, O LORD,
>> for I call to you all day long.
>
> vv. 1–3

■ Today's Truth: John 15:4–5, 7–8, 11; 1 John 2:27

Remain in me, and I will remain in you. No branch can bear fruit by itself; it must remain in the vine. Neither can you bear fruit unless you remain in me. I am the vine; you are the branches. If a man remains in me and I in him, he will bear much fruit; apart from me you can do nothing. . . . If you remain in me and my words remain in you, ask whatever you wish, and it will be given you. This is to my Father's glory, that you bear much fruit, showing yourself to be my disciples. . . . I have told you this so that my joy may be in you and that your joy may be complete.

John 15:4–5, 7–8, 11

As for you, the anointing you received from him remains in you, and you do not need anyone to teach you. But as his anointing teaches you about all things and as that anointing is real, not counterfeit— just as it has taught you, remain in him.

1 John 2:27

A branch cannot bear fruit apart from the vine any more than a hair dryer can dry hair apart from being hooked up to a power source. Jesus said we are like the branches attached to the vine (the power source of Christ himself). When we are not connected, we are void of power and fruit. But when we are connected, all things are possible in and through us. When connected, we can operate as the manufacturer intended.

I don't know the plans God has for me; I just know he does have plans. I also know that I have tried in my own strength to live as a "good Christian woman" and failed. Just throw me a curve ball in life, and all bets are off when operating on my own.

But when I am connected to my maker, his power pulsing through me, my life is filled with the very things I so desperately desire: love, joy, peace, patience . . . anyone else need these?

Funny thing is, you cannot buy these things. They come from the Holy Spirit. You cannot spray the Holy Spirit on like perfume in the morning. You must be connected to Jesus to bear the fruit of the Holy Spirit in your life.

How do we connect?

- We connect to Christ through prayer . . . talk to him!
- We connect to Christ through his Word . . . listen to his viewpoint!
- We connect to Christ through fellowship . . . learn from those in your circle!
- We connect to Christ through obedience . . . God is pleased with faith and when we walk it out in our lives in baby steps, big steps, or any steps!

I have found that it's important for me to connect first thing in the morning. As I open my sleepy eyes, I begin with an immediate prayer of surrendering myself to God that day. I ask to be connected to his power and to be equipped to follow his purpose and plan for me that particular day. Even if my day just has grocery shopping on the agenda, I still connect with Christ. From that point on, it seems I am more attuned to listen for him, look for him, and be drawn to the awareness of him in my midst. It is amazing how such a simple thing can start the day off differently.

When I remain in him, a very real anointing gives me power to live. In this authentic encounter with God, I no longer need to rely on counterfeits and impostor power. I can relax, remain in him, and be renewed in him. In this place I can hardly wait to read his Word and just be with him. Coffee with Jesus is one of my favorite things. I sit before him and he just blows me away . . . with his power, presence, and love.

Today's Dare: Plug into the Power Source

- Stop right now and plug into the source of all power, Jesus Christ. Do this by getting away from everything for a moment and coming to Jesus in prayer and handing every part of you over to him.
- Ask to be cleansed from your sin and filled anew with his Spirit.
- Now read today's Scripture passages again, this time out loud. Spend some time thinking about what connection means in your everyday reality.
- Dare to step out of your comfort zone today. Dare to try something you would not ordinarily feel you could do. Experience the power of God enabling you to live above yourself.

Journal

Acknowledging where we are is the first step to living in faith and truth.

Today's truth is speaking to me . . .

_____

_____

_____

_____

_____

_____

_____

God is asking me to . . .

_____

_____

_____

_____

_____

_____

My challenge is to . . .

_____

_____

_____

_____

_____

■ Today's Prayer

Father, blow me away as I connect to you. Be my power, the rhythm of my life, the cadence of my steps, and everything that represents me walking here on this earth. Live in me, work through me, have your intended way in my life today, tomorrow, next week, next month . . . always, Lord. I desire to remain in you and be blown away by your power, presence, and love.

You did not choose me, but I chose you and appointed you to go and bear fruit—fruit that will last.

John 15:16

■ Today I Believe . . .

When I am connected to the power source of all life, good fruit will characterize my life and God-appointed things will happen in and through me.

Day 9

Asking and Not Receiving

*Dare to Remember That God Gives
Good Gifts to His Children*

Call to me and I will answer
you and tell you great and
unsearchable things you do not
know.

Jeremiah 33:3

Troubled is a perfect word to describe how I felt after months
of joining one of my children in prayer over a certain situation.
I went back to the verses I had been claiming, words of Christ:
ask, seek, and knock. I had done all three. I struggled as I reread
the Scripture passage because I hadn't received an answer, hadn't
found anything but disappointment, and the door I had knocked
on was closed shut.

My inner dialogue with the Lord went something like this:
"Why? I am sincerely trying to follow your Word . . . asking instead of worrying, knocking in trust on your door. So why?" I was
frustrated, but then the answer came and rocked my thoughts. As

I was led to reread the passage in context, the verses that followed opened up a new understanding for me: stand in truth today and rejoice. God gives good gifts. God gives bread not a stone. Your prayers will be answered from on high because your good God has heard every one. The doors knocked on will be opened, but only when it's safe to open them and only when it's time for you to receive what is behind the door. God is good. Claim it, stand in it, thank him for it. Rejoice today that you have a God who loves you more than anyone could ever love you.

■ Today's Praise/Prayer: Psalm 116

> I love the LORD, for he heard my voice;
>   he heard my cry for mercy.
> Because he turned his ear to me,
>   I will call on him as long as I live. . . .
>   I was overcome by trouble and sorrow.
> Then I called on the name of the LORD:
> "O LORD, save me!"
>
> vv. 1–4

■ Today's Truth: Matthew 7:7–11

> Ask and it will be given to you; seek and you will find; knock and the door will be opened to you. For everyone who asks receives; he who seeks finds; and to him who knocks, the door will be opened. Which of you, if his son asks for bread, will give him a stone? Or if he asks for a fish, will give him a snake? If you, then, though you are evil, know how to give good gifts to your children, how much more will your Father in heaven give good gifts to those who ask him!
>
> Matthew 7:7–11

My aha moment came as I reread these verses thousands of feet in the air in midflight on a recent trip. I wanted to tell everyone on the plane what came to me at that moment. Instead, I will tell you.

I had asked, sought, and knocked . . . for months. Every time I got frustrated I was led back to the fact that it was good that I was asking, seeking, and knocking on God's door! The fact that I hadn't gotten the answer I was looking for did not mean God hadn't heard or hadn't answered. Rather, he was preventing my child from getting a stone or a snake instead of bread. In other words, God has something good for my child and will answer my prayers on his behalf. The answer will come in God's time because everything is about a bigger picture. But surely in God's time the answer will come in the form of a good gift. Whether it is the answer I wanted or expected is not important; the important thing is that God will give the right gift and answer to prayer at the right time.

God is love and God is good. He cannot work in any way except that which expresses who he is and is in line with his character. So I can relax and trust a good God and his answers and timing.

I am still waiting, still seeking, still knocking . . . but now I am also praising. Why? Because even though I don't see the answer today, I know it's coming. It's coming in the form of God's good and perfect will. God will give my child bread, not a snake or a stone . . . and in this I rejoice!

Today's Dare: Remember That God Gives Good Gifts to His Children

- Today believe that God has heard your prayer and is working in his timing.
- Thank God for the thing you have prayed for but have not yet received.
- Thank him that he has only good gifts for you. If your prayer is unanswered, then the good gift just isn't there yet—it's not right, not time.
- Turn your thinking around about time lines and learn to trust in God's time.

- Dare yourself to praise God each time you worry today over the prayer for which you do not presently see an answer.
- Dare yourself to speak the truth each time you think of your prayer: that God has heard and will give his answer in the form of a good gift in his timing.
- Remind yourself that you are God's child, and he gives his children good things.

Journal

Acknowledging where we are is the first step to living in faith and truth.

Today's truth is speaking to me . . .

_____

_____

_____

_____

_____

_____

_____

_____

God is asking me to . . .

_____

_____

_____

_____

_____

_____

_____

_____

_____

My challenge is to . . .

_____

_____

_____

_____

_____

Today's Prayer

> *Father, help me in my disappointment and unbelief. I choose today to thank you for bread, good answers, and good timing. I choose to trust that doors will open when it's safe and time for them to open. I choose to trust that you are the sovereign controller of circumstances.*

For the pagans run after all these things, and your heavenly Father knows that you need them.

Matthew 6:32

Today I Believe . . .

I have a heavenly Father, and he knows what I need and provides all I need.

Day 10

Mind Management

Dare to Guard Your Thoughts and Fill Your Mind with Good

Set your minds on things above, not on earthly things. For you died, and your life is now hidden with Christ.

Colossians 3:2

We have flies everywhere. Last August it was ants; this summer it's flies. We left the sliding door open for the dogs, and the flies made themselves right at home. Having flies camping out on your hands or buzzing around your face is disgusting, annoying, and downright frustrating. Last night as I tried to fix dinner, the flies were all around me. I lost my appetite and gave up. It was the topper to an already crummy day.

Then I realized I had felt like giving up all day. Troubling thoughts, like flies, had buzzed around my mind all day long—defeating thoughts, discouraging thoughts, "everybody hates me" thoughts!

All day I had been thinking about something I was going through. I did look up with the problem a few times, and doing so helped get me through the next hour. But as the day wore on, I got tired of shooing away the bad thoughts, and at some point they overtook me. I got really discouraged.

The bad thoughts took over just like the flies. You see, at first there was just one fly. Not so bad. Before long there were two, then four, then an army of flies in my house. Yuk! I swatted them when it was manageable, but as their army increased, I gave up and left my post (the kitchen).

Bad thoughts are like flies. They dog us, change the way we view things, and come in like a swarm to discourage us.

Focus is a key element in living up in relationship to God. It takes focus on him to live differently. Giving over my circumstances has everything to do with my mind and what I allow in and out of it each day. I am often challenged with something I call "mental moments"—moments when I am going a little mental as I spiral down a path of negative thinking, buying into thoughts that are the opposite of God's Word, or taking a simple problem and over-thinking it into a giant mental firestorm.

It is clear to me that I must give my thoughts to God. The best way to stop a mental moment is to interrupt it and replace it with a positive truth, a Scripture passage, or praise. This interruption is an important spiritual discipline we must practice and learn.

▪ Today's Praise/Prayer: Psalm 3

> But you are a shield around me, O LORD,
>   my Glorious One, who lifts up my head.
> To the LORD I cry aloud,
>   and he answers me from his holy hill.
> I lie down and sleep;
>   I wake again, because the LORD sustains me.
> I will not fear the tens of thousands
>   drawn up against me on every side. . . .

From the LORD comes deliverance.

May your blessing be on your people.

vv. 3–6, 8

■ Today's Truth: Romans 8:6; 2 Corinthians 10:3–5; Philippians 4:8; Colossians 3:2

To be carnally minded is death, but to be spiritually minded is life and peace.

Romans 8:6 NKJV

For though we live in the world, we do not wage war as the world does. The weapons we fight with are not the weapons of the world. On the contrary, they have divine power to demolish strongholds. We demolish arguments and every pretension that sets itself up against the knowledge of God, and we take captive every thought to make it obedient to Christ.

2 Corinthians 10:3–5

Finally, brothers, whatever is true, whatever is noble, whatever is right, whatever is pure, whatever is lovely, whatever is admirable—if anything is excellent or praiseworthy—think about such things.

Philippians 4:8

Set your minds on things above, not on earthly things.

Colossians 3:2

As Christians we are different. I realize I keep repeating this fact, but it bears repeating. Why? Because different people are called to different lives. We are not just human-flesh people anymore; we are born-of-the-Spirit and filled-with-God people—though we still live in human-flesh bodies and live with human-flesh problems. God's Word is the divine power that can demolish the places in our minds that are held in a stranglehold by our own negative thoughts, worldly perceptions, or the lies of hell. We cannot huff and puff and blow away the bad thoughts. But we must take them captive, making them obedient to truth.

In his book *The 4:8 Principle*, Tommy Newberry says, "The battle you wage against in your human nature is an invisible one that will be won or lost in the mind. Minute by minute, hour by hour, in the hidden workshop of your mind you are constructing thoughts of good or evil, depression or joy, success or failure. You are writing your own life story as a human being with each subtle and soundless thought you think."[1]

The best way to get rid of bad thoughts is to replace them with whatever is good. It sounds simplistic, but it really works. If there is any good, choose to dwell there. Stay in the positive. Fill your mind with what is good, and the peace of God will be yours.

I like to think of this mind management as a treasure hunt. Approach your thoughts as one who is looking for treasure in the middle of a field. You are on the lookout for anything good, anything beautiful. Once you find it, stay there, stay with that thought, idea, reasoning.

Here's how it works. A habit of your husband's is driving you crazy. You keep thinking about it. That's when you take action. You begin an exercise of stopping the negative thought. "I will not dwell on the bad in my husband." You search your mind for something good. "He is a good provider, and I am cared for." Though this might not have anything to do with the original negative thought, it is positive and now becomes the focus of your thought. This is managing what you think. No one can control where you dwell mentally except you.

In the moment that God tests your faith the longest and the deepest, don't run away or turn your back on him. Rather, reach up and throw your arms around his neck and ask him to show you his mercy, compassion, and loving-kindness because that is who he is.

And when the lies that he is something different or that he is not there for you buzz around your pretty little head, get out the lie swatter of God's Word and hit those pesky lies. They are lies. Shoo them away. Don't walk away from your post like I walked away from the kitchen. Shoo them away and get back to the business of living in Christ.

■ Today's Dare: Guard Your Thoughts and Fill Your Mind with Good

- Recognize the negative thoughts and determine how regularly you entertain them.
- Practice putting a positive where a negative might be.

Negative	Positive
My kids are brats.	I am blessed to be a mom.
I have no money.	I have a roof over my head and food to eat.
I hate my hair.	I have hair and can find new ways to do it.
I hate my thighs.	I am healthy and can work at improving.
My husband is inattentive.	I am grateful to have a husband and will show him that.
I feel terrible.	It could always be worse.
My life is hard.	God is shaping me to be more like him.

- Guarding your mind means putting up barriers of truth in it so that when the negative thoughts come, you have something with which to combat them. Each hour, on the hour, stop and thank God for something positive in your life.

■ Journal

Acknowledging where we are is the first step to living in faith and truth.

Today's truth is speaking to me . . .

_____

_____

_____

_____

_____

_____

_____

God is asking me to . . .

_____

_____

_____

_____

_____

_____

_____

My challenge is to . . .

_____

_____

_____

_____

_____

Today's Prayer

> *Father, I come to you knowing that it is important to surrender my mind to you. This means that when I have negative thoughts that threaten to take me away from my place of peace in you, I have to do something. Teach me how to cast down, tear down, or disassemble every thought that does not honor you or your Word.*

107

For your name's sake, O LORD, preserve my life;
   in your righteousness, bring me out of trouble.
In your unfailing love, silence my enemies;
   destroy all my foes,
   for I am your servant.

Psalm 143:11–12

■ Today I Believe . . .

When I focus my thoughts on the good, my mind is at peace.

Live In! In Surrender of Self

And so, dear brothers and sisters, I plead with you to give your bodies to God because of all he has done for you. Let them be a living and holy sacrifice—the kind he will find acceptable. This is truly the way to worship him. Don't copy the behavior and customs of this world, but let God transform you into a new person by changing the way you think. Then you will learn to know God's will for you, which is good and pleasing and perfect.

Because of the privilege and authority God has given me, I give each of you this warning: Don't think you are better than you really are. Be honest in your evaluation of yourselves, measuring yourselves by the faith God has given us.

Romans 12:1–3 NLT

Each day we choose how to live. We choose our own way or God's way. We also choose to go through life or grow through it—we can thrive or survive. This part dares us to choose complete, focused surrender.

> The choice that will be continually before you: either to live the Christian life in your own power and ability and end up crashing and burning like so many other Christians you see today; or learn to set yourself aside and let Christ live His Life out through you.
>
> The result of living the Christian life in your own power and ability is hypocrisy and as Deuteronomy 30:19 says, "death and disaster." The result of letting Christ live His Life out through you *is real Christianity* and the genuineness and freedom that everyone is truly seeking.[1]

Day 11

A Different Life

Dare to Live No Longer for Self

I no longer live, but Christ lives in
me. The life I live in the body, I
live by faith in the Son of God,
who loved me and gave himself
for me.

Galatians 2:20

She didn't want to obey. She thought following God was getting tiring and becoming a bit of a pain. My friend looked at me, worn-out and frustrated, as she boldly exclaimed, "I just don't want to do it. I have a say, I have rights, I will do what I want to do, when I want to do it!" I understood the stand she was making, and I also understood the rebel in each of us who doesn't want anyone telling us what to do—not even God. When we try to protect ourselves, we often put up walls that keep even God's voice out. We want to do things our way, and he will let us do just that.

We were created for something bigger and better than our way. But self-preservation comes naturally to us. Being in control is a key component in a woman's life, and when we feel out of control, we

111

are not very happy. These things have been ingrained in us since we were young, and because they come naturally they seem okay. But the normal Christian life is not what we call normal today. The saints of old strained toward a different kind of life. The love of Christ influenced them in such a dramatic way that they no longer desired self-interests. They longed for the interests of God instead.

What if we laid ourselves aside? What if we believed, really believed, that God's love is powerful enough to protect us, keep us, and guide us into everything we will ever need in our lifetime? What if, because of this love, we began to live differently than anything we ever imagined?

These questions are answered throughout Scripture—through stories and promises and the words of Jesus himself. Words such as, "I am the bread of life. He who comes to me will never go hungry" (John 6:35). "I am the good shepherd. The good shepherd lays down his life for the sheep" (John 10:11). "No one can snatch them out of my hand" (John 10:28). "I have come that they may have life, and have it to the full" (John 10:10).

Full life. Abundant life. We have heard about it, but it often seems more like an elusive promise than a reality we can live in. And therein lies the problem: the basics of the faith have become so common to us that they have lost their power to move us. Do you want to be set free to live a different life? Then you must go back to the basics, the essentials of faith, and learn what it means to put all your faith in the truths represented there. Look at each daily dare as a way back to the basics. Celebrate change!

■ Today's Praise/Prayer: Psalm 23

> GOD, my shepherd! I don't need a thing.
> You have bedded me down in lush meadows,
>   you find me quiet pools to drink from.
> True to your word,
>   you let me catch my breath
>   and send me in the right direction.

Even when the way goes through
    Death Valley,
I'm not afraid
    when you walk at my side.
Your trusty shepherd's crook
    makes me feel secure.
You serve me a six-course dinner
    right in front of my enemies.
You revive my drooping head;
    my cup brims with blessing.
Your beauty and love chase after me
    every day of my life.
I'm back home in the house of GOD
    for the rest of my life.

vv. 1–6 Message

■ Today's Truth: John 10:10–11; 2 Corinthians 5:14–15

The thief comes only to steal and kill and destroy; I have come that they may have life, and have it to the full. I am the good shepherd.

John 10:10–11

A thief is only there to steal and kill and destroy. I came so they can have real and eternal life, more and better life than they ever dreamed of. I am the Good Shepherd.

John 10:10–11 Message

For Christ's love compels us, because we are convinced that one died for all, and therefore all died. And he died for all, that those who live should no longer live for themselves but for him who died for them and was raised again.

2 Corinthians 5:14–15

The most important things we need to understand about Christ/ the Good Shepherd are these:

113

- He loves us deeply and unconditionally.
- He wants the best life for us and is always working in our lives, even when life is difficult.
- He will never leave us or forsake us.
- He is committed to providing for us, caring for us, and leading us to the pasture that is best for us.
- He understands our temptations and weaknesses and sympathizes with us.
- He invites us to enter into his love for us and be changed by it.
- He invites us, through his death on the cross, to live now in his power.
- He came to give us the best life, a full life—which might not be a life of ease but a life of peace and blessed spiritual substance.

The most important things we need to understand about our enemy/the thief are these:

- He does not love us but masquerades as a lover.
- He does not want the best life for us and is always trying to trip us up.
- He doesn't care about our welfare and just wants to hold on to us for his own kingdom's victory.
- He is constantly trying to destroy, steal, or kill any good thing in our lives.
- He will try to make sure we see our lives as empty rather than full, because he does not want us to trust in the living God.

Let's face it: we like to think abundant life is about having everything go our way. It's much easier to have a fully devoted heart when everything is fine. But what about when we have bad news, a bad day, or conflict? Part of living with an undivided heart is learning to live well even when the sky is falling—especially then! It's time to battle through our moods, feelings, and attitudes to the point of complete faith in our Lord Jesus Christ. Oswald Chambers says it like this:

> Faith is not some weak and pitiful emotion, but is strong and vigorous confidence built on the fact that God is holy love. And even though you cannot see Him right now and cannot understand what He is doing, you know Him. The real meaning of eternal life is a life that can face anything it has to face without wavering. If we will take this view, life will become one great romance—a glorious opportunity of seeing wonderful things all the time. God is disciplining us to get us into this central place of power.[1]

I once heard it said that this kind of faith is like breaking out of our own little world of experience and living in abandoned devotion to him. Abandoned devotion . . . I like that.

To live well we must have a core allegiance to something. This means we must choose one of the following:

- self and all its interests, dreams, and concerns
- the approval of others, seeking to meet all their expectations first and foremost
- the culture and what is popular, trendy, expected, and valued by our overall society
- God and all that he is, all that he is doing, where he is leading and working

■ Today's Dare: Live No Longer for Self

- Ask God to show you how you can experience abundance by living differently in the most practical areas of life.
- Ask for the grace to live bigger than the smallness of yourself.
- Thank him all day that he is able to lead you and guide you into what is best for your life.

- Trust him for strength in the areas that tempt you to live in ways that are not God's best for you.
- Give him the details that are heavy on your heart and thank him for the advantage of his presence and power working on your behalf.
- Praise him over and over today for being your Good Shepherd.
- Think about his love. Quiet yourself in the truth of God's love for you.
- Dare to run back to a place of stillness, even mentally, many times today.

Journal

Acknowledging where we are is the first step to living in faith and truth.

Today's truth is speaking to me . . .

_____

_____

_____

_____

_____

_____

God is asking me to . . .

_____

_____

_____

_____

_____

_____

My challenge is to . . .

_____

_____

_____

_____

_____

▪ Today's Prayer

> *Jesus, I often forget that you are the Good
> Shepherd—not just any shepherd but my Good
> Shepherd. Thank you that you desire to offer mercy,
> grace, and compassion to me. I sometimes feel
> ashamed of what I am feeling or thinking, and so
> I keep it to myself rather than bringing it to you.
> Remind me to bring everything before you, because
> you desire to bring me to a place that is bigger than
> just me and filled completely with you. Thank you for
> leading me to what is best for me.*

> In repentance and rest is your salvation,
>   in quietness and trust is your strength. . . .
> The LORD longs to be gracious to you;
>   he rises to show you compassion. . . .
> Blessed are all who wait for him! . . .
> How gracious he will be when you cry for help!
>
> Isaiah 30:15, 18–19

▪ Today I Believe . . .

It is better to live for Christ than stay stuck in self. The Lord, my
Shepherd, longs to be gracious to me!

Day 12

Woman of Worth

Dare to Believe You Are God's Treasure and of Great Value to God

> God, your God, chose you out of all
> the people on Earth for himself as
> a cherished, personal treasure.
>
> Deuteronomy 7:6 Message

We put so much value on externals—what we do, what we wear, what we have, and what we accomplish. This is shallow value. The rich, full life that Christ has for us is more secure than the flimsy appearance model that spells worth in our culture. Our worth has been sealed by God. He created us, planned for us, and ordained our days.

He set us apart from birth, carries us through life, and holds us this moment. He will never lay us down, put us down, or separate us from his love. He has called us his woman, his treasure, his holy people, and the sheep of his pasture. He has called us daughter, friend, bride, and beloved. His goodness and love follow us, chase after us—and find us again and again. We are not subject to the standards of this world, unless we choose to be. We now live by a different standard, a different authority, and a higher power. We are the people of God. The challenge is, do we believe it?

Today's Praise/Prayer: Psalm 4

> Know that the LORD has set apart the godly for himself;
>   the LORD will hear when I call to him. . . .
> You have filled my heart with greater joy
>   than when their grain and new wine abound.
> I will lie down and sleep in peace,
>   for you alone, O LORD,
>   make me dwell in safety.
>
> vv. 3, 7–8

Today's Truth: Deuteronomy 7:6; Psalm 139:14; Isaiah 46:3–4

For you are a people holy to the LORD your God. The LORD your God has chosen you out of all the peoples on the face of the earth to be his people, his treasured possession.

Deuteronomy 7:6

I praise you because I am fearfully and wonderfully made;
  your works are wonderful.

Psalm 139:14

Listen to me, O house of Jacob . . .
you whom I have upheld since you were conceived,
  and have carried since your birth.
Even to your old age and gray hairs
  I am he, I am he who will sustain you.
I have made you and I will carry you.

Isaiah 46:3–4

As long as we are searching for significance and value in things other than our Creator, we will always be searching. We will never

119

be full but always empty. This isn't to say there aren't blessings in life, for certainly there are. And this isn't to say that significant relationships don't add value to the story we are living. But Scripture teaches that we come from a place of worth and value. God values those whom he has made. This is evidenced throughout Scripture, but unfortunately it usually goes unnoticed in our lives.

There is a saying that God doesn't make junk. I have no idea who thought of that, but it's funny and makes me smile. Unfortunately, I have spent a significant amount of my life thinking I'm not worth much. I am not sure where those beliefs came from—maybe from a critical mother, or the shame of not feeling like I fit in or was enough. Perhaps it was because I was the last pick for the team and not the prettiest girl in the class. Who knows. All I know is that now I realize that the thief, the enemy of my soul, was working on me long before I realized it. He wanted me to believe I was worthless so that I would live as if I were worthless.

You see, this enemy is threatened by us when we realize our worth because confidence in God and his work in us is much different from prideful self-confidence. God-confidence causes us to rise above ourselves and live in him. God-confidence causes us to be grateful for the gift of value bestowed upon us and the gift of grace that leads us each day. God-confidence causes us to trust that we are his, we are beautiful in his sight, and we are chosen for his plan. God-confidence causes us to bow our hearts humbly before the one who says, "You are my girl, my love, my treasure."

I have an acronym for woman:

W—wonderful worth
O—ordained for God's purposes
M—managing life by faith
A—attitude of thanks and praise
N—nearer to God each day

120

The first two points are the foundations of truth: we are his wonderful work, and he values us and has a design and intent for our lives. From this starting point we build a life: we can manage all that comes our way through faith in God, with a new attitude of praise in all things, while growing nearer to him each day.

For the record, your enemy, the thief, hates all this. He wants you to think you are worthless. It's a lie. The truth stands: you are precious, loved, and valued.

■ Today's Dare: Believe You Are God's Treasure and of Great Value to God

- Today believe the truth that you are valuable to God.
- What is your birth date? Recognize it as the day that God began your story here on earth. Get out a childhood photo and thank him for creating you.
- Ask God to heal you from the negative messages that have made you feel you have little value or little to contribute.
- Make a list of the natural things God put within you that others recognize as positive traits or gifts.
- Commit yourself and that list to God, and be thankful for who you are and whose you are.
- Tell yourself the truth: I am fearfully and wonderfully made, I am his, I am his treasure, I am his possession.
- Think about the people in your life—your inner circle. Picture them in your mind, realizing that just as you are God's treasure so are they. What could you do today to express to them that they are valuable to you and to God?

■ Journal

Acknowledging where we are is the first step to living in faith and truth.

Today's truth is speaking to me . . .

_____
_____
_____
_____
_____
_____
_____

God is asking me to . . .

_____
_____
_____
_____
_____
_____

My challenge is to . . .

_____
_____
_____
_____
_____

Today's Prayer

Lord, worth is an interesting thing. It is measured in many ways and measured differently by many people. Worth to you is measured in who you see when you look at me. You see the woman you created, and you see the death of Christ, which redeemed me and made me new. You see creation and you see re-creation. You see Christ and you see

*the cross. Help me to see me the way you see me,
and in seeing the truth may I settle into my worth as
your treasure.*

All things were created by him and for him. He is before all things, and in him all things hold together.

Colossians 1:16–17

■ Today I Believe . . .

God made me to use me as he has planned. He goes before me and holds me together.

Day 13

Bringing Beauty to Life

Dare to Surrender to the Process of Change

> Those who look to him are radiant;
> their faces are never covered with
> shame.
>
> Psalm 34:5

We walked into the store—a fancy pearl shop on a casual Hawaiian island. The pearls in each showcase were beautiful and came in several colors and sizes. In the spirit of Hawaii the local merchant told us the story behind the pearls, and as I listened to something I thought I already knew, I realized that this little stop in the pearl shop was teaching me about spiritual matters. God was talking to me about myself, about his shaping process. I am his very own pearl in the making.

The story goes . . . pearls are formed one irritating grain of sand at a time. I was told it takes five years of this kind of irritant to create the black pearls I was admiring. Five years? Irritation? Hmmm. We can learn much about God through nature. Jesus taught through word pictures such as the branch on the vine and the fruit on a tree. Now I was getting a clear picture of a woman in process, subject to thing after irritating thing, as God shapes me and changes me from day to day, glory to glory. This change is part of the rich, full life that makes up the substance of abundant living.

We are changed daily in small steps and in unseen ways. This daily change happens through the surrender of our will to God. God is not destroying our will but rather transforming it as he changes us into all he has planned us to be.

Today's Praise/Prayer: Psalm 91

"Because he loves me," says the LORD, "I will rescue him;
    I will protect him, for he acknowledges my name.
He will call upon me, and I will answer him;
    I will be with him in trouble,
    I will deliver him and honor him.
With long life will I satisfy him
    and show him my salvation."

vv. 14–16

Today's Truth: Isaiah 61:1–3; Galatians 2:20; Hebrews 12:1–2

He has sent me to bind up the brokenhearted,
    to proclaim freedom for the captives
    and release for the prisoners . . .
to comfort all who mourn . . .
to bestow on them a crown of beauty
    instead of ashes,
the oil of gladness
    instead of mourning,
and a garment of praise
    instead of a spirit of despair.

125

> They will be called oaks of righteousness,
> a planting of the LORD
> for the display of his splendor.
>
> Isaiah 61:1–3

I have been crucified with Christ and I no longer live, but Christ lives in me. The life I live in the body, I live by faith in the Son of God, who loved me and gave himself for me.

Galatians 2:20

Let us throw off everything that hinders and the sin that so easily entangles, and let us run with perseverance the race marked out for us. Let us fix our eyes on Jesus, the author and perfecter of our faith.

Hebrews 12:1–2

Scripture is clear: my life is not my own. Scripture is also encouraging: God's life in me brings out the beauty of his creation. He takes broken hearts and heals them, messy lives and mends them, tears and dries them. He dresses me in something new and beautiful. The clothing is from within, but its beauty is seen without. It's always been his plan to renew me, revive me, restore me, and give me courage to quit living my life in my own flimsy, fleeting beauty and to live in him and the beauty of his holiness.

Oh, that we might realize this truth as women today: it's not supposed to be about us. We are free to take a backseat and let God drive our life and our days. We no longer live—Jesus lives in us and has plans to live through us. And because of this truth we are to untangle ourselves from the world and engage ourselves in Christ and his life in us. We are to focus our eyes on one target, one goal, one love—Jesus.

It is time to believe that the shame that has covered us or the insecurity that has surrounded us can be changed by looking to Christ. It is with this upward gaze that we are changed and no longer ashamed. So take an inward look at the hurt that seems to be holding you back, mentally place it in your hands, and lift that hurt to the God who loves you. Then believe his Word: you are radiant.

Today's Dare: Surrender to the Process of Change

- Throw off all that hinders you (stop and think about what this is asking of you).
- Say no to the sin that has you tangled in knots (the first thing that came to your mind).
- Run the race that is marked out for you (don't run anyone else's marathon, only yours).
- Fix your eyes on one focus only: Jesus (he wants to be your everything).
- Refocus and rethink as often as needed throughout the day.
- Thank God that he is busy bringing his beauty to life in your life—beauty from ashes.
- Dare yourself to be part of someone else's healing. What can you do to help restore the beauty of a broken friend or relative? What practical act can you do today that expresses, "Jesus loves you and so do I"?

Journal

Acknowledging where we are is the first step to living in faith and truth.

Today's truth is speaking to me . . .

_____

_____

_____

_____

_____

_____

God is asking me to . . .

_____

_____

_____

_____

_____

_____

My challenge is to . . .

_____

_____

_____

_____

Today's Prayer

Lord, I long for your Spirit's present-tense power. I want the indwelling life of Christ to be my greatest reality. Teach me to focus on the truth that Christ is in me. Thank you for being the restorer of all that has been lost and broken in my life. Thanks that you use the brokenness to make me more beautiful. Oh, you are an amazing God—wasting nothing, using everything, writing my story as I live in you.

The kingdom of heaven is like a merchant looking for fine pearls. When he found one of great value, he went away and sold everything he had and bought it.

Matthew 13:45–46

Today I Believe . . .

Jesus gave his life for me, laid down everything he had, so that I might be reconciled to God through his death. His death at work in me brings beauty to life.

Day 14

Not Enough

*Dare to Believe You Were
Not Created to Be Enough in Yourself*

He has made us competent
[adequate, enough, sufficient].

2 Corinthians 3:6

Jackie looked at me with tears in her eyes. "I am haunted by two words, and they are controlling everything I do." She wiped away a trickle of fresh tears. "Not enough is like a silent mantra of my soul. I can't escape them, and I am dying under the shame of them." I understood exactly what she was talking about because I too lived for a long time with those two words. Today I am recovering from the effects of a life lived with the silent refrain, "Not enough."

Those two words made their way to my heart when I was very young. I didn't know how to articulate them, process their meaning, or understand what they were doing within me. From the time I was about ten years old, I was always trying to be more, be better, try harder, and be enough to be okay. I used to think it was just me, but I have come to realize that "not enough" is an epidemic among women. Christian women have it worse because they want to be enough in their practical lives as well as in their spiritual lives. This inner refrain is destructive to the beauty God is bringing forth within us. As long as we are trying to be enough, we will be chronically about self and not about God. We will do whatever we need to do to protect self instead of dying to self in favor of living for God.

Chronic insecurities keep us at arm's distance from others, and believe it or not, they can keep us at a distance from God. It's not God who moves but us. We distance ourselves without realizing it, believing we will never be enough anyway. Some women quit trying, quit daring to be all that God has planned for them to be. When this happens, the thief has won. He celebrates, and we suffer the sad reality that what once was a light of hope in the promise of Christ has been reduced to a dependence on self to try to make us good enough to be in Christ.

News flash! Becoming enough on our own is not God's plan for us. He never created us to be enough. He wants us to know we are enough—because of him and his life in us.

▪ Today's Praise/Prayer: Psalm 34

> I will extol the LORD at all times;
>> his praise will always be on my lips.
> My soul will boast in the LORD;
>> let the afflicted hear and rejoice.
> Glorify the LORD with me;
>> let us exalt his name together.
> I sought the LORD, and he answered me;
>> he delivered me from all my fears.
> Those who look to him are radiant;
>> their faces are never covered with shame.

vv. 1–5

Today's Truth: 2 Corinthians 3:4–6, 12, 17–18

Such confidence as this is ours through Christ before God. Not that we are competent to claim anything for ourselves, but our competence comes from God. He has made us competent as ministers of a new covenant—not of the letter but of the Spirit; for the letter kills, but the Spirit gives life.

2 Corinthians 3:4–6

Therefore, since we have such a hope, we are very bold.

2 Corinthians 3:12

Now the Lord is the Spirit, and where the Spirit of the Lord is, there is freedom. And we, who with unveiled faces all reflect the Lord's glory, are being transformed into his likeness with ever-increasing glory, which comes from the Lord, who is the Spirit.

2 Corinthians 3:17–18

I could barely contain my delight when I realized that it was never God's plan for me to be enough within myself. I could quit stressing over that and instead look to him. He would be enough in me, for all things, at all times. His Spirit, which is powerful within me, would change me, transforming me from a woman of self-focus and insecurity to a woman of God-focus and confidence.

The word *competent* in 2 Corinthians 3:4–6 is from the Greek *hikanos*, which means good, worthy, sufficient, adequate, or enough. So in living in truth I can say:

- I am not good in and of myself.
- I am not worthy in and of myself.
- I am not sufficient for God's purpose in and of myself.
- I am not adequate for a God-sized life in and of myself.
- I am not enough in and of myself.

God didn't create us to be confident in who we are. He created us to rely on him and look to him for our confidence, competence, and significance. I like how Max Lucado says it: "What makes us special is . . . the signature of God on our lives."[1]

God is our letter of recommendation, and he is forever writing our story.

■ Today's Dare: Believe You Were Not Created to Be Enough in Yourself

Think about the following questions: If I believed I am enough because Christ lives in me and makes me enough . . .

- How would I view myself differently?
- If I viewed myself differently, would I live a different kind of life?
- What risks would I take that I don't take now?
- Would I be less afraid and more daring to follow Christ?
- Would I trust him to do things through me that I never dreamed I could do?
- Would I quit putting myself down?
- Dare to refuse any negative thought about yourself or any negative self-talk for the next twenty-four hours. Be as kind to yourself as Christ is to you.

■ Journal

Acknowledging where we are is the first step to living in faith and truth.

Today's truth is speaking to me . . .

_____

_____

_____

_____

_____

God is asking me to . . .

_____

_____

_____

_____

_____

_____

_____

My challenge is to . . .

_____

_____

_____

_____

_____

Today's Prayer

> *Dear Jesus, I know that for years I have believed I needed to do more to be enough. This is the message of the culture I live in. I want to be freed from this self-focus and the insecurity it produces in me. I want to understand the significance of your life within me. I want more than anything to be changed into your likeness and to live in the confidence that in you I am enough for anything and everything you have mapped out for my life.*

The king is enthralled by your beauty.

Psalm 45:11

▪ Today I Believe . . .

When God looks at me, he sees beauty—the miracle of his creation.

Day 15

He Completes Me

Dare to Believe You Are Complete in God

Now the Lord is the Spirit, and
where the Spirit of the Lord is,
there is freedom.

2 Corinthians 3:17

When Tom Cruise said, "You complete me," to Renée Zellweger in the movie *Jerry Maguire*, every woman in the audience melted. Why? Because we all want to be loved like that. We long for it in friendship, in romance, and even in motherhood. We are searching for that person or those people who will complete us, making anything resembling half in us a beautiful whole.

But what if we believed it is Christ who completes us? Or that we actually are complete because of Christ in us and his work for us? Could it be that this kind of love is the very thing that makes us balanced, centered, secure, and yes . . . complete?

If we believed we are complete in Christ, we could stop our search for something more and could begin living life. Gone would be the five steps to success, the speedy plan for getting our acts together, or the fool-proof plan for a better life. We could stop feeling needy and move into a place of confidence. Realizing we are complete in Christ makes all that he is doing in us worth some of the pain—because in the end the maturity and wholeness will be the spiritual gain.

There is freedom in embracing the truth that all we are and all we ever will be is now hidden in Christ and constructed by the power of Christ's work in us.

■ Today's Praise/Prayer: Psalm 8

> O LORD, our Lord,
>> how majestic is your name in all the earth!
> You have set your glory
>> above the heavens.
> From the lips of children and infants
>> you have ordained praise
> because of your enemies,
>> to silence the foe and the avenger.
> When I consider your heavens,
>> the work of your fingers,
> the moon and the stars,
>> which you have set in place,
> what is man that you are mindful of him?
>
> vv. 1–4

■ Today's Truth: Acts 17:24–25, 28; 2 Corinthians 4:7; Colossians 2:10

> The God who made the world and everything in it is the Lord of heaven and earth and does not live in temples built by hands. And he is not served by human hands, as if he needed anything, because he himself gives all men life and breath and everything else. . . . "For in him we live and move and have our being." As some of your own poets have said, "We are his offspring."
>
> Acts 17:24–25, 28

But we have this treasure in jars of clay to show that this all-surpassing power is from God and not from us.

2 Corinthians 4:7

And in Him you have been made complete, and He is the head over all rule and authority.

Colossians 2:10 NASB

Isn't it interesting that *complete* means perfect or perfected? Even more interesting, we are not made perfect in ourselves but in Christ. We wear ourselves out trying to perfect ourselves, but the truth is, in Christ we are made perfect and complete. How can this be? He does not judge perfection the way we do. Perfect in a spiritual sense is one who is being completed through maturity, growth, and surrender to God.

Wives: You have all that is necessary to love your husband in a way that will be meaningful to him and pleasing to God. Come to Christ daily for your complete filling of all you need for this calling. Ask God to love this man through you.

Mothers: You are complete in Christ. You have already been given all you need to be the mother that your child/children need. Come to Christ daily and be filled. God has a plan for each life created; you are in partnership with God in the development of human lives. This is a high calling.

In the workplace: You have all that you need to get along with people, live in integrity, and be a light. You are also made complete for the task as you trust Christ in you. God put you right where you are; trust him to give you success in your line of work and to work through you. Be diligent.

In ministry: You cannot go another day without claiming your competence and completion in Christ! You cannot change a life; you are not the Messiah. But you are a Jesus follower and a difference maker because of him. Come daily and be filled with his power, making you complete, whole, and ready for what he calls you to do in service for that day.

All of life is ministry, so all of us, regardless of life vocation, season, or position, need to be filled and ready to live a life of completion by Christ's power each day.

Today's Dare: Believe You Are Complete in God

Ask the following questions:

- What if Christ wasn't just a complement to your life but a completion of all you were made to be?
- What if because of the presence of his Spirit in you, you were complete to do all and to be all that he has planned for you to do and be?
- What if you were secure because Christ is your completion and you were made more than enough in him?
- What if a change took place at the most fundamental level in you, the places you cannot see, when his Spirit came to make a home in you?
- What if Christ, making himself real in you, completed you to the point of being valuable for his work as an ordinary woman made extraordinary by his presence and power?
- Dare to see Christ in yourself and then to turn the light of truth on the way you view others. Today look at others through the lens of Christ desiring to be their all, to complete them, and to make them extraordinary in Christ.
- Pray for every family member today who is not a Christian. Ask God to draw them to the truth, and ask God to fill you with truth so that you will be able to tell them about their significance from God's perspective.

Journal

Acknowledging where we are is the first step to living in faith and truth.

Today's truth is speaking to me . . .

_____

_____

_____

_____

_____

_____

_____

God is asking me to . . .

_____

_____

_____

_____

_____

My challenge is to . . .

_____

_____

_____

_____

■ Today's Prayer

Father, thank you for your work on the cross, a sacrifice that often seems so academic to me. Make it a real-life part of my belief system. I don't know how to embrace or believe the significance of this on my own. Work your truth in me. By faith I thank you that I am complete in you and I am enough, competent, adequate, sufficient for all you have called me to do, because you complete me!

139

Finally, brethren, rejoice, be made complete, be comforted, be like-minded, live in peace; and the God of love and peace will be with you.

2 Corinthians 13:11 NASB

◼ Today I Believe . . .

God completes me!

Day 16

A New Attitude

Dare to Choose Whom You Will Serve
and the Direction You Will Take

Be joyful always; pray continually.

1 Thessalonians 5:16

It's 6:00 a.m. and I am out in my backyard letting my two little dogs do their thing. This morning the sky looks like a watercolor portrait in shades of gray, promising that rain is on its way. It's lovely but gloomy. Yet, high upon my second-story roof sits a bird singing, singing, singing. It's beautiful. He is up there closer to those storm clouds than I am, and he is singing with all his might, chirping away a song like only a bird can chirp. The moment is priceless.

Once again I see why Jesus used the birds as an illustration of carefree trust. While I am disappointed that it's going to rain today, the bird is taking it all in and singing his song to me. What would it be like if we were so confident in Christ's care that we sang in the middle of our gloomy days and our painful moments?

A few months ago a friend of mine had the perfect opportunity to choose joy. Shattered glass covered her driveway like a blanket of glistening lights. The neighbor boy did not mean for his baseball to go through the windshield of her brand-new car, but it did. Should he have been more careful? Sure. Was it an accident? Yes. Did he feel terrible? You bet. Did my friend want to wring his little neck? Yep. But she didn't.

She was learning, once again, that not everything that happens in life is good. But regardless of what happens, God is still working in it. If we look to him, we will find strength for the hard things, patience in the daily things, and joy in all things.

You see, it's easy to take the right faith steps when things are good and life is clicking along at a steady, routine pace. But what about the times when glass covers the driveway, a friend betrays you, your boss overlooks you, or your house is going into foreclosure? What about those times?

When bad things happen, everything we believe in is tested. Our surrender to a good God is threatened by the things we can't understand, fix, or control. And yet the nature of surrender is to let go and let God have everything that concerns us. It helps if we learn to believe, at the very core of us, that no matter what, we are in good hands.

■ Today's Praise/Prayer: Psalm 138

> Though the LORD is on high, he looks upon the lowly,
>   but the proud he knows from afar.
> Though I walk in the midst of trouble,
>   you preserve my life;
> you stretch out your hand against the anger of my foes,
>   with your right hand you save me.
> The LORD will fulfill his purpose for me;
> your love, O LORD, endures forever—
>   do not abandon the works of your hands.

vv. 6–8

■ Today's Truth: Romans 8:28–29; Hebrews 12:1–2, 5–7, 10–13

> And we know that in all things God works for the good of those who love him, who have been called according to his purpose. For those God foreknew he also predestined to be conformed to the likeness of his Son.
>
> Romans 8:28–29

> Let us run with perseverance the race marked out for us. Let us fix our eyes on Jesus, the author and perfecter of our faith. . . . Do not make light of the Lord's discipline and do not lose heart when he rebukes you, because the LORD disciplines those he loves. . . . Endure hardship as discipline; God is treating you as sons. . . . God disciplines us for our good, that we may share in his holiness. No discipline seems pleasant at the time, but painful. Later on, however, it produces a harvest of righteousness and peace for those who have been trained by it. Therefore, strengthen your feeble arms and weak knees. "Make level paths for your feet," so that the lame may not be disabled, but rather healed.
>
> Hebrews 12:1–2, 5–7, 10–13

During the faith dare we have challenged ourselves to believe in God's bigger plan, his greater love, and our choice to surrender to that plan. Scripture tells us that God foreknew us and that he planned for us to be conformed to the likeness of his Son.

In Romans 8 Paul starts out by talking about living life differently . . . in the Spirit. After Paul explains the difference between living in the flesh and living in the Spirit, he talks about our identity as God's children, and then he goes right to our present sufferings. He encourages us by saying that the Spirit helps us in our weakness and that all of these sufferings, trials, and hardships are working together for our good . . . *because* it is God's will to conform us to the image of his son. My take on all of this: things happen *to* us, so something can happen *in* us.

Today I want us to consider the choice to respond to truth while in the middle of pain, trials, sufferings, and hardships. There is a reason Jesus told us to look at the birds (see Matthew 6). The birds are carefree, and Jesus says we too can be carefree. How? How can we be carefree in a life filled with cares, sufferings, injustices, hardships, and pain? By making a choice to fix our eyes on Jesus and to find purpose in the pain by allowing God to teach us the truth of being conformed to his image.

- All of us have a path, a race, a route mapped out for us.
- We are to run it, live in it, with perseverance.
- Embrace the Lord's discipline, because there is a purpose in the pain.
- The purpose is good, because the purpose is that we share in his holiness.
- In the moment, pain. Later on, peace.

What is your pain today? Can you turn it around from being just a life circumstance that is horrible to a life event that God has allowed for your good and growth? If growth is the outcome, can you begin to hope for something better than you currently have? Can you place yourself, your pain, and your circumstance into the hands of the God who calls you his daughter? Can you believe that this God who created you is not like an earthly father but a Father who always and only wants your good and growth? Can you trust that he is the beginning and ending of all things, knows the bigger picture of your life, and therefore works all things to fit into the bigger picture? Can you join me today in fixing our eyes on Jesus?

My friend has a necklace that speaks to me. The front side says, "Choose Joy," and the back side says, "Never look back." I think that is what Hebrews 12 is saying to us today. Choose joy because God is working, and never look back because you cannot run the race while looking behind you.

Run the race! It's a choice to lace up those shoes and run. Can you make that choice today? Choose to run. Choose to endure. Choose joy in God's bigger plan!

Today's Dare: Choose Whom You Will Serve and the Direction You Will Take

- Considering truth, make a choice to make a level path for your feet as you run the race.
- Clear the path, make it level, by focusing your eyes and attention on Jesus and putting your trust in him in the midst of your pain. Dare to identify the thing that is not necessary in your life right now and eliminate it to clear the path ahead of you.
- Believe that this pain will produce righteousness in your life in practical ways.
- Believe that this pain will produce peace and will train you for the life you were born to lead.
- Believe that this present pain is working to make you more like God's Son, Jesus.
- What do you perceive God might be testing in you as a result of your current situation? Dare to believe that God is good and that he is always working for the good.
- Dare to choose a bigger-picture attitude all day today. That means staying focused on the plan of the big picture of your life, a plan you may not be able to see with your eyes but must trust with your heart.

Journal

Acknowledging where we are is the first step to living in faith and truth.

Today's truth is speaking to me . . .

_____
_____
_____
_____
_____
_____
_____
_____

God is asking me to . . .

_____
_____
_____
_____
_____
_____

My challenge is to . . .

_____
_____
_____
_____

▪ Today's Prayer

Father, I am weak and, yes, sometimes emotionally feeble. Change me. Give me the courage to fix my attention on the bigger picture, the greater good, and on you. Jesus, I want to be conformed to your image. Give me the grace to endure whatever it is that is taking me there.

146

Consider it pure joy, my brothers, whenever you face trials of many kinds, because you know that the testing of your faith develops perseverance.

James 1:2

Today I Believe . . .

Whenever life is hard, God has a plan. I will look to God and count each circumstance a gift.

Day 17

The Mirror Image

Dare to Live in the Miracle of Who You Are

By the grace of God I am what I am.
1 Corinthians 15:10

We have all seen the mirrors in a carnival fun house. The distortions can turn our bodies into something pretty scary or pretty skinny. We laugh; it's all in good fun. Real mirrors often aren't fun because we bring our own distorted images of ourselves with us. Often, distorted thinking about who we are warps how we view ourselves. Rather than seeing the miracle God created, we see a distorted and shame-based woman who is not perfect, who is ashamed of her imperfections, and who is chronically trying to see herself differently by changing the external. The merry-go-round of self-loathing is too common and is once again the thief who robs us of life.

From the time we are young we want to know three things:

Who am I?
Why am I here?
Where am I going?

And as we grow up we long for significance, appreciation, acceptance, and love. Many women wonder if their lives have meaning and purpose. Many more women spend their lives trying to get better and better in the hope that if they become good enough, purpose will find them.

If we don't know at the core level who we are and why we are here, we will remain forever lost in the search for significance, which seems to keep us lost in self. So beginning today, let's turn this around. Let's firmly plant ourselves in some core Scripture passages about our beginning and about our significance. In doing so we will have a solid foundation whenever the thief tries to rob us of our true God-given identity.

■ Today's Praise/Prayer: Psalm 139

> For you created my inmost being;
>> you knit me together in my mother's womb.
> I praise you because I am fearfully and wonderfully made;
>> your works are wonderful,
>> I know that full well.
> My frame was not hidden from you
>> when I was made in the secret place.
> When I was woven together in the depths of the earth,
>> your eyes saw my unformed body.
> All the days ordained for me
>> were written in your book
>> before one of them came to be.

vv. 13–16

■ Today's Truth: 2 Corinthians 5:16–17

So from now on we regard no one from a worldly point of view. Though we once regarded Christ in this way, we do so no longer. Therefore, if anyone is in Christ, he is a new creation; the old has gone, the new has come!

1 Corinthians 5:16–17

149

Because of this decision we don't evaluate people by what they have or how they look. We looked at the Messiah that way once and got it all wrong, as you know. We certainly don't look at him that way anymore. Now we look inside, and what we see is that anyone united with the Messiah gets a fresh start, is created new. The old life is gone; a new life burgeons!

2 Corinthians 5:16–17 Message

We don't see things the way God sees them. We look at ourselves and see our mistakes. God looks at us and sees his purpose and the miracle of himself in us. It's easy to take our life for granted, and when we do, we rarely live on purpose. Instead, we live just to get by or to make ourselves more significant. Truth is, you can't possibly be more loved or significant than you are at this very moment. You don't have to be doing something to be significant; significance comes from being somebody. You already are somebody—a woman created by God for his purposes.

■ Today's Dare: Live in the Miracle of Who You Are

- When you look in the mirror today, see God's daughter looking back at you.
- Get out a childhood picture of yourself and put it somewhere prominent this week. Make it your facebook profile picture, screen saver on your computer, or tape it somewhere you will see it. Each time you see it remind yourself that though you were created by God and born into this world as someone's child, you have been born again into a spiritual reality. You are no longer who you once were.
- Tell yourself these answers to life's questions:
  - » Who am I? I am God's daughter, loved, cherished, and kept by the Good Shepherd.
  - » Why am I here? I have been created by God and for him, to love him and love others.

150

» Where am I going? God determines my days and the places I will live. He is accomplishing all things in my life so that my life will conform completely to his will.

Journal

Acknowledging where we are is the first step to living in faith and truth.

Today's truth is speaking to me . . .

_____

_____

_____

_____

_____

_____

_____

_____

God is asking me to . . .

_____

_____

_____

_____

_____

_____

_____

My challenge is to . . .

_____

_____

_____

_____

_____

■ Today's Prayer

Lord, life seems to be a constant back-and-forth
struggle as I grow up in you. One day up, the next
down. Help me to stay connected to the truth that
you live in me and want me to be set apart so that
wherever I am you can do your will through me. Take
your Word, which is living and active, and plant the
truth of who I am deep in my heart. Help me to live
in the miracle of who I am.

For we are God's workmanship, created in Christ Jesus to do good
works, which God prepared in advance for us to do.

Ephesians 2:10

■ Today I Believe . . .

I am God's work. I have been re-created spiritually in Christ. God
has plans for my life.

152

Day 18

Get Out of the Funk

Dare to Live with a New Focus

Let the peace of Christ rule in your
hearts.

Colossians 3:15

Your day starts out fine, but then before you know what hit you, you find yourself in a funk. You are feeling emotional, discouraged, out of sorts, even a little depressed.

What if we could learn to get ourselves out of the funky places we get ourselves into? You know what I am talking about—that emotional place where the world seems to spin out of control. We all find ourselves there from time to time. Stephen Arterburn speaks of his own struggle when he says:

> In my own life, when I am in the middle of a crisis, I have a pretty dismal view of the future. It is mostly full of fear, anxiety, and dread. I reach a point where I don't think I can take any more and will do anything to avoid feeling more pain or enduring another struggle.

153

I see only the doom and gloom hovering around my life. If there is an upside, I can't see it and don't believe it is there.[1]

Webster's defines the word *funk* as a cowering fear or a dejected mood. The definition of *funky* is to be overcome with great fear, terrified, or having a bad smell. I had to laugh at the definitions because truth be told, when I am in a funk, my attitude stinks! How about you?

Here is my own acronym of FUNK:

F—focus problem; feelings prevail

U—under the circumstances, under the conditions, under the weather

N—needy

K—keeping the fire of the funk burning by tending to it, keeping it alive

The funk always starts with a focus problem. Every emotional hole of despair we find ourselves in usually starts with a circumstance that disrupts our faith focus. Once our focus is skewed, we begin to spin out of control. Instead of living above our circumstances as an overcomer, we begin to live down under the mess. In this place we become scared, insecure, needy, and dependent on circumstances getting better or people fixing things for us.

Today's Praise/Prayer: Psalm 34

> I will extol the LORD at all times;
> > his praise will always be on my lips.
> My soul will boast in the LORD;
> > let the afflicted hear and rejoice.
> Glorify the LORD with me;
> > let us exalt his name together.
> I sought the LORD, and he answered me;
> > he delivered me from all my fears.

Those who look to him are radiant;
    their faces are never covered with shame.

vv. 1–5

■ Today's Truth: Hebrews 12:2–3

Let us fix our eyes on Jesus, the author and perfecter of our faith, who for the joy set before him endured the cross, scorning its shame, and sat down at the right hand of the throne of God. Consider him who endured such opposition from sinful men, so that you will not grow weary and lose heart.

Hebrews 12:2–3

How do we fix our eyes on Jesus to regain a healthy focus? Fix:

- to repair, mend
- to put in order, adjust, or arrange
- to make firm or stable
- to place definitely and more or less permanently
- to settle definitely
- to direct the eyes or attention
- to hold the eye or attention in one place

I have worn corrective lenses since my early twenties. I am amazed how much my vision can mess me up. When I have the wrong prescription glasses, when my contacts are clouded, or when a lens is scratched or dirty, I see things differently. When I don't see correctly, I get a headache and feel "off " all day long. Our vision is extremely important to our physical well-being.

In the same way, our spiritual and emotional vision is important to our spiritual and emotional well-being. I think we can all agree that our eyes, our focus, our attention are often in need of repair. We scatter our focus every which way, and when we need to focus on Jesus and his faithfulness, we get distracted. We need to learn how to fix our eyes on Jesus. This alone will help significantly with the funk. As the rest of today's verse says, when we focus on Christ, consider him, we will not grow weary or lose heart. Much funk involves losing heart, weariness, and attention and focus on the wrong thing . . . the negatives.

Today consider this question: how can I fix my eyes on Jesus?

A funk cannot start unless we have a focus problem. We like to blame our funk on someone else or on our circumstances. But the truth is no one can put you into a funk. A funk happens when you lose perspective by losing focus. As Christians this focus problem happens when we take our eyes off Jesus and the faithful God he is and choose to muddle along in our problems, focusing on how bad things are or seem to appear. In this place we do not have our eyes and attention fixed on Jesus. We have our eyes and attention fixed on self.

What's a girl to do? Focus, focus, focus. You are in the Father's hand and nothing can snatch you from this place. When the funk threatens to take you down, look up. When your emotions start churning within, look up. When life gets you down, look up to the God who picks you up!

■ Today's Dare: Live with a New Focus

- Take your position as a woman who belongs to God.
- Stand firm, being solid in who you are and whose you are.
- He will save you. Get up and out of that foul emotional place. God is with you.
- Don't be afraid. It's a scary, wild world, but God is bigger and wilder in power!
- Do not lose hope. Redirect your focus on the one who is faithful.

- Go out and face the day. Face each day in Christ's strength with the hope that he is with you.
- Dare to make any decision that will get you up and out in order to have a change of focus. Pray and ask God to show you the reason you are in a funky place, allow you to learn from it, and help you out of it.

■ Journal

Acknowledging where we are is the first step to living in faith and truth.

Today's truth is speaking to me . . .

_____

_____

_____

_____

_____

_____

God is asking me to . . .

_____

_____

_____

_____

_____

_____

My challenge is to . . .

_____

_____

_____

_____

_____

■ Today's Prayer

Lord, you are the Lord of freedom, of life, and of liberty, not the Lord of the funk. Help me to learn how to recognize it when it's coming, guard against it when I am tempted to slip, and stand firm in my position as a person loved by you!

Indeed, the very hairs of your head are all numbered. Don't be afraid; you are worth more than many sparrows.

Luke 12:7

■ Today I Believe . . .

God knows me completely and loves me totally. I no longer have to spiral down to the places that are funky and depressing.

Day 19

Live as an Overcomer

Dare to Get Your Head Out from under the Circumstances

> [Jesus said,] "In this world you will have trouble. But take heart! I have overcome the world."
>
> John 16:33

Today let's look at the next letter in funk, the *U*—under. Under the circumstances, under the condition of my problem, under the weather. When living under the problem of the day, we will find ourselves crushed by the weight of the circumstance. With our focus off our faithful God, we move into the place of living under the problem and the weight of the emotion associated with it. This results in anxieties of all kinds.

Do you really think it is God's best for you and me to live *under* things?

Don't get me wrong, we will go *through* things in this life, but do you think we are to be *under* them?

■ Today's Praise/Prayer: Psalm 142

> I cry aloud to the LORD;
>> I lift up my voice to the LORD for mercy.
> I pour out my complaint before him;
>> before him I tell my trouble.
> When my spirit grows faint within me,
>> it is you who know my way.

vv. 1–3

■ Today's Truth: John 16:33; Romans 12:21; 1 John 5:4

I have told you all this so that you may have peace in me. Here on earth you will have many trials and sorrows. But take heart, because I have overcome the world.

John 16:33 NLT

Don't let evil conquer you, but conquer evil by doing good.

Romans 12:21 NLT

For every child of God defeats this evil world, and we achieve this victory through our faith.

1 John 5:4 NLT

We can live under . . . it's been done before; it's nothing new. Take a look at what the psalmist said about that: "Remove your scourge from me; I am overcome by the blow of your hand" (Ps. 39:10). The Amplified Bible says, "I am consumed by the conflict."

We all know how to be consumed by the conflict, don't we? When we focus only on self and become consumed by the conflict, we begin to live under it rather than being an overcomer through faith in Christ.

Again, you cannot blame the funk on anyone else. You are agreeing to be there by staying in your self and refusing to live as an overcomer. I realize this is hard to swallow. It's hard for me to swallow too.

Just this week I found out that I have a potentially serious health issue. I can live under the fear of it, or I can keep my eyes on Jesus. I admit that in this situation living under fear will get me more attention and sympathy. But I don't want sympathy; I want Jesus. I want to live above the circumstance, stay out of the funk, and keep my eyes on Jesus, the author of my life and the finisher of my faith. If I choose to be in a funky place, that is my choice. But it will not be a good choice.

What will you choose?

God gives us many opportunities to practice walking out our faith and establishing our beliefs through our circumstances. Today is another opportunity for you and for me. I choose today to be positive, to walk in the faith that God knows me and loves me and that I am in his hand.

Will you join me in the walk of faith? Will you join me in believing that God is involved in our daily lives? Will you join me in learning to live *over* our circumstances to the glory of God?

Today's Dare: Get Your Head Out from under Your Circumstances

- Dare to have a positive stance regarding your current problem.
- Focus your eyes on Jesus and your faith in him.
- Do not focus on what you feel in the middle of the situation. Do not allow the conflict to consume you.
- Find ways to live over, not under.
- Find something good you can do just for today that will overcome the negative and give you a positive to think about.

161

Journal

Acknowledging where we are is the first step to living in faith and truth.

Today's truth is speaking to me . . .

_____
_____
_____
_____
_____
_____
_____

God is asking me to . . .

_____
_____
_____
_____
_____
_____

My challenge is to . . .

_____
_____
_____
_____
_____

Today's Prayer

Father, it is so easy for me to settle down under my problem, without even thinking about your power to help me rise above. When I do so, I am not living in faith but in unbelief. Help my unbelief and teach me how to be an overcomer in you.

Do not worry about tomorrow, for tomorrow will worry about itself. Each day has enough trouble of its own.

Matthew 6:34

Today I Believe . . .

I do not have to live under my problems in worry. I can trust that God will get me through each day and each life circumstance.

Day 20

Needy, Whiny, and Discouraged

*Dare to Speak Praise, Sing Praise,
and Live with Confidence in God*

Give thanks in all circumstances, for
this is God's will for you.

1 Thessalonians 5:18

The funk begins with a focus problem, and soon we travel down a path of living under our circumstances rather than overcoming them. The *N* stands for being needy and the *K* for keeping the funk alive.

When we are under our problems, we become a bit whiny and needy. In this place we become discouraged, and our bad attitude keeps the fire of the funk burning. But there is a way out: learn the power of praising God in all things.

Praising God will change your life! I realize it sounds simplistic, but it is a powerful biblical truth that we don't dare ourselves to live in often enough. A young woman recently told me that when people act like that they are just "blowing sunshine," and it's not real. How sad to think that even in church we have become suspicious of anyone who is positive! We are much more comfortable with discouraged or negative people. We have come to expect people to live in turmoil.

It's not enough to redirect our focus and affirm with our minds and hearts that God loves us. Those two things are very important, but we can't stop there. We also need to look at how whiny and needy we have become while living so much of life for self or within the confines of insecurity about self. This type of life is not God's abundant best for us.

Constant complaining only serves to keep the negative fire burning brightly. It's time to put out the fire's flame. Don't fan it. Put it out!

How? Turn your attitude around! Anyone can whine. But it takes a different kind of woman who wants to live a different kind of life to turn whining into thankfulness instead. Look for the good. Thank God for anything that might be good. If your *situation* is not good, then thank God that *he* is.

As I wrote this I decided to start a gratefulness journal. It will be a special journal for the season I am in. I will use it to praise God and to remind myself to thank God each day as I go through a change in my life. It will remind me to be in touch with life, love, hope, and spiritual health. Praising God will:

- help me live above my circumstances
- train me to set my heart and mind on things above
- set up an ambush for the enemy
- enable me to live differently than if I just went along my funky way

What battle do you face today? How has life hit you in a way that makes you want to crawl under the covers and hide? You don't have to hide, and neither do I. We can go out and face the day, face our battles, and face our disappointments. How? By taking our positions and standing firm. What is our position? Our position, according to Scripture, is one of being God's dearly beloved child. As his child, we have received his Holy Spirit to lead us, empower us, and comfort us through the hard times in this life. The Lord will save us. The Lord is for us. We do not have to live in a place of discouraged neediness. We can live as a daughter of the King! Take your position today and stand firm in who you are and whose you are.

We have the power and freedom in Christ to choose something different each time life gets us down. It will take some practice, because for some of us whining has become very familiar. But with a little practice and some time, we can learn to live in a healthier place. Come out, bow your heart before God, begin praising him because he is good!

■ Today's Praise/Prayer: Psalm 125

> Those who trust in the LORD are like Mount Zion,
>> which cannot be shaken but endures forever.
> As the mountains surround Jerusalem,
>> so the LORD surrounds his people
>> both now and forevermore.

vv. 1–2

■ Today's Truth: 2 Corinthians 2:14; Ephesians 3:14–19; 1 John 4:18

> But thanks be to God, who always leads us in triumphal procession in Christ and through us spreads everywhere the fragrance of the knowledge of him.

2 Corinthians 2:14

> I ask him to strengthen you by his Spirit—not a brute strength but a glorious inner strength—that Christ will live in you as you open the door and invite him in. And I ask him that with both feet planted firmly on love, you'll be able to take in with all followers of

166

Jesus the extravagant dimensions of Christ's love. Reach out and experience the breadth! Test its length! Plumb the depths! Rise to the heights! Live full lives, full in the fullness of God.

Ephesians 3:14–19 Message

There is no room in love for fear. Well-formed love banishes fear. Since fear is crippling, a fearful life—fear of death, fear of judgment—is one not yet fully formed in love.

1 John 4:18 Message

Inner strength is God's best for us. According to truth, having inner strength is his will for us. And his will does not add up to being needy, whiny, and discouraged all day long! Just look at what Paul prayed for the church in Ephesus. He asked that they

- be strengthened by Christ's Spirit
- gain glorious inner strength
- yield to Christ's authority
- plant both feet firmly on Christ's love
- live a full life from this position

God always leads us in a procession of triumph. He spreads the fragrance of his beauty and love through us. There is no room for fear, for living in fear cripples this full life. When we are discouraged and stay there, the fragrance is not of life but of fear and death.

What if your troubles today are forming inner strength in you for tomorrow? Remember, you are being led in a procession of triumph in Christ, right now, troubles and all.

Today's Dare: Speak Praise, Sing Praise, and Live with Confidence in God

- Start today by thanking God that he is with you and he is leading you.

167

- Begin a gratefulness journal. This can be elaborate if you love the journal idea, or it can simply be a calendar where you write down things you are thankful for each day.
- Next, thank God that he is producing inner strength in you.
- Finally, ask him to plant your feet firmly on the belief that he wants what is best for you, that he is your heavenly Father and loves you, and that he will never leave you . . . even in trouble.
- Dare to say "thank you" or "I praise you, Jesus" several times throughout the day.

Journal

Acknowledging where we are is the first step to living in faith and truth.

Today's truth is speaking to me . . .

_____
_____
_____
_____
_____
_____
_____

God is asking me to . . .

_____
_____
_____
_____
_____
_____

My challenge is to . . .

_____

_____

_____

_____

_____

■ Today's Prayer

> *Lord, I come today and confess that I whine. I am*
> *sorry. I want to learn how to praise more than whine*
> *and complain. I am realizing that when I whine I am*
> *showing an absence of trust in you. Lead me in your*
> *way, in my mind and with my mouth.*

For it is God who works in you to will and to act according to his
good purpose.

Philippians 2:13

■ Today I Believe . . .

God is working in me and his work is good—this is my confidence
in all situations.

Live Out! In Relationship to Others

This is how we've come to understand and experience love: Christ sacrificed his life for us. This is why we ought to live sacrificially for our fellow believers, and not just be out for ourselves. If you see some brother or sister in need and have the means to do something about it but turn a cold shoulder and do nothing, what happens to God's love? It disappears. And you made it disappear. My dear children, let's not just talk about love; let's practice real love. This is the only way we'll know we're living truly, living in God's reality.

1 John 3:16–18 Message

If we are serious about following after God, then we must become students of the way he expressed himself in relation to others. Jesus had a style. He was a servant—living the love of God out in practical ways. He was a lover—living the truth of the way God values people through respecting them and caring for them. He was a giver—providing what was needed, when it was needed. He was a restorer—giving grace in the moment and covering a bunch of sins and shortcomings through the power of God's love.

We will never be Jesus, but we are followers and as his children learn to live a life that is not self-focused but rather that extends beyond the confines of self into the heart and needs of other people.

> From the beginning of time God has created us for relationship with Himself and relationship with each other—but things have gotten in the way. It started with Adam and Eve in that beautiful Garden of Eden. Pride got in the way; they did their own thing and disobeyed God. Then they blamed each other and ultimately hid from God. Sometimes we aren't much different! Like Eve we take the bait, make a selfish choice, blame everyone else, and then hide from God and others as our relationships crumble around our feet. Thankfully, God in His love sent the answer by sending His Son Jesus. From the point of salvation until the day we take our last breath, each of us needs the power of God to live in the rich, full life that has been designed for us from the beginning of time—a life of relationship with God and others.[1]

All of us need love, acceptance, and forgiveness. Allow your faith in Christ to translate into love for others!

Day 21

Keep Yourself in God's Love

Dare to Love Well

> Build yourselves up in your most
> holy faith. . . . Keep yourselves
> in God's love as you wait for the
> mercy of our Lord Jesus Christ to
> bring you to eternal life.
>
> Jude 20–21

Do you want to live the fullest life possible? Living well has many facets, but a primary biblical component to living well is loving well. According to Jesus, the two most important things in life are to love him with all our heart, soul, and strength and—second to that—to love others. With that one statement from the lips of the Savior, we are given a life mission statement that is biblically correct but personally challenging:

I am to live to love God.
I am to live to love others.

Simply stated, but not simply lived. Loving others is not as poetic and lovely as it sounds. Loving would be easy if we could just stay hidden away in a cave, but we can't. Loving other people involves other people—and therein lies the problem. We cannot control people—their moods, attitudes, reactions, and decisions. People hurt us, and we hurt them. The cycle repeats, and we get defeated. Some of this hurt is what keeps our hearts divided, closed off, and fragmented. Hurt can be the culprit of hearts that are no longer centered on God's love but rather focused on self-preservation. There is a better way to live. Start today by looking up and praising God aloud while reading today's psalm.

■ Today's Praise/Prayer: Psalm 1

> Blessed is the man
>   who does not walk in the counsel of the wicked
> or stand in the way of sinners
>   or sit in the seat of mockers.
> But his delight is in the law of the LORD,
>   and on his law he meditates day and night.
> He is like a tree planted by streams of water,
>   which yields its fruit in season
> and whose leaf does not wither.
> Whatever he does prospers.
>
> vv. 1–3

■ Today's Truth: Matthew 5:8–9, 43–48; 1 Corinthians 13:4–8

Blessed are the pure in heart, for they will see God. Blessed are the peacemakers, for they will be called sons of God. . . . You have heard that it was said, "Love your neighbor and hate your enemy." But I tell you: Love your enemies and pray for those who persecute you, that you may be sons of your Father in heaven. . . . If you love those who love you, what reward will you get? Are not even the tax collectors doing that? And if you greet only your brothers, what are you doing more than others? Do not even pagans do that? Be perfect, therefore, as your heavenly Father is perfect.

Matthew 5:8–9, 43–48

Love is patient, love is kind. It does not envy, it does not boast, it is not proud. It is not rude, it is not self-seeking, it is not easily angered, it keeps no record of wrongs. Love does not delight in evil but rejoices with the truth. It always protects, always trusts, always hopes, always perseveres. Love never fails.

1 Corinthians 13:4–8

Jesus is asking us to live in his love and love with his love. Love is who he is; it is the description of what he stands for. He was strong yet gentle, firm yet loving—grace and truth—and an example of how to live.

Jesus shook people up. His style was not that of the natural man. The natural man loves to receive love back, gives to get back, and lives in a conditional reality. Jesus spoke against that. He taught radical responsibility for your own self, your own heart, and your own actions. He gave no outs or excuses when it comes to the people who wrong us. He taught us to love because God himself created all and re-created us in Christ Jesus that we can live a new and different life in him.

In Matthew 5:48 the word *perfect* means be mature. Jesus taught that the road to a mature and complete life involves doing things differently, viewing life and people through his lens. He taught that to live well (mature and complete) we have to make a decision to love well. And it all started with, "Blessed are the pure in heart, for they will see God" (Matt. 5:8).

Why do we continue living the way the world does?

Why do we continue to contribute to the cycle of hurting others and loving them less than God taught us to?

Today's Dare: Love Well

- Ask God to show you the areas that need healing in your relationships.
- Recognize the reasons people usually love less (jealousy, hurt, being offended, being competitive, pride) and choose not to make their personal issues yours.
- Get real about the reasons you have been loving less. Take personal responsibility.
- Commit someone to God whom you do not especially like or do not currently care about. Ask God to change your attitude.
- Pray for a person today who comes to mind who has hurt you.

Journal

Acknowledging where we are is the first step to living in faith and truth.

Today's truth is speaking to me . . .

_____

_____

_____

_____

_____

_____

_____

God is asking me to . . .

_____

_____

_____

_____
_____
_____
_____

My challenge is to . . .

_____
_____
_____
_____
_____
_____

Today's Prayer

> *Lord, I want to come into agreement with the truth. I desire to be pure in heart, and I want to learn to live according to the Jesus style of living. I don't know how to love my enemies. My own hurts get in the way, and my selfish heart cries out for love. When I am loved, I want to love back. But when I am not loved, I want to hurt back. I see today that you want me to love first regardless of the outcome. You have given me a new heart. Teach me how to love and show me when I am loving less than your best for me. I want to learn your ways.*

> Hear my voice when I call, O Lord;
>   be merciful to me and answer me. . . .
> Do not hide your face from me,
>   do not turn your servant away in anger;
>   you have been my helper.
> Do not reject me or forsake me,
>   O God my Savior.

> Though my father and mother forsake me,
> the LORD will receive me.

Psalm 27:7, 9–10

■ Today I Believe . . .

The Lord is my helper and will teach me how to love others when I would rather hold back.

Day 22

Forgiveness

Dare to Practice Forgiveness,
Speak Forgiveness, and Choose Forgiveness

Whoever claims to live in him must
walk as Jesus did.

1 John 2:6

I have been hurt many times. After being burned over and over again, I could easily believe the words of Christ are no longer relevant to real life. Why should we forgive others? After all, they don't change. How can God expect us to put up with them?

Jesus said we are to forgive. Quite frankly, I often don't want to. But he went as far as saying that if we do not forgive, we will not be forgiven. Sounds to me like he was making a serious point. Yet forgiveness is often misunderstood, leaving people feeling like they shouldn't do it, can't do it, or haven't done it. This tangled web is exactly what Satan loves to create in believers' lives. If he can get us confused, then we will put off doing what is right, live in shame over how we think we should be doing it, or walk away from the subject!

■ Today's Praise/Prayer: Psalm 143

> The enemy pursues me,
>> he crushes me to the ground;
>> he makes me dwell in darkness
>> like those long dead.
> So my spirit grows faint within me;
>> my heart within me is dismayed.
> I remember the days of long ago;
>> I meditate on all your works
>> and consider what your hands have done.
> I spread out my hands to you;
>> my soul thirsts for you like a parched land.
>> Selah
> Answer me quickly, O LORD;
>> my spirit fails.
>> Do not hide your face from me
>> or I will be like those who go down to the pit.
> Let the morning bring me word of your unfailing love,
>> for I have put my trust in you.
>> Show me the way I should go,
>> for to you I lift up my soul.
> Rescue me from my enemies, O LORD,
>> for I hide myself in you.
> Teach me to do your will,
>> for you are my God;
>> may your good Spirit
>> lead me on level ground.

vv. 3–10

■ Today's Truth: Luke 6:37

> Forgive, and you will be forgiven.
>
> Luke 6:37

Forgive in the Greek language is *aphiemi*, which can be translated as lay aside, forsake, leave, let go, let alone, omit, yield up, put away.

180

The confusion over forgiveness comes in two ways.

1. We think we have to receive an apology to forgive. I don't see this in Scripture, do you?
2. We think we haven't forgiven if we still remember the offense. Scripture doesn't say to forget but to forgive, which is to lay aside the offense.

Think how difficult it would be if forgiving required totally forgetting. I don't think that could happen without a frontal lobotomy!

Just because we abstain from chocolate or our favorite food for a season doesn't mean we forget what it tastes like. The way it tastes is in our memory even though we are not currently digesting the food. In the same way, an offense will most likely be in our memory, but when we have forgiven or laid it aside, we are not digesting, internalizing, or holding tight to the hurt anymore. In other words, though we remember we were offended, we are no longer currently living in the offense. We have laid it aside and given it up, because Jesus said this is the way to live.

It takes courage to follow Jesus, and forgiveness is an example of courage.

It takes courage to offer an apology, and Jesus asks us to set things straight on our end.

It takes courage to let go and trust God.

Will you join me in seeking to be a courageous Christian woman whose faith is not based on emotional feelings but on what Jesus taught, how Jesus lived, and on the blood Jesus shed?

▪ Today's Dare: Practice Forgiveness, Speak Forgiveness, and Choose Forgiveness

- Consider who is hanging around in your mind because you haven't let that person go and turned the offense you experienced over to God.

- See if there is anything you believe about forgiveness that might be skewed or might be keeping you at arm's length from true spiritual/emotional/mental freedom.
- If you need to forgive someone, consider writing a letter or setting up a time to meet. Ask God; he will guide you.
- Sometimes we forgive from our heart, and the other person doesn't even know anything is going on. If someone is in your mind today, dare to let go of how that person has affected you.
- Dare to make a step toward forgiveness.
- Make a decision today to quit speaking negatively about the person who hurt you—speaking only positively about that person or not speaking about him or her at all.

Journal

Acknowledging where we are is the first step to living in faith and truth.

Today's truth is speaking to me . . .

_____
_____
_____
_____
_____
_____

God is asking me to . . .

_____
_____
_____
_____
_____
_____

My challenge is to . . .

_____

_____

_____

_____

_____

■ Today's Prayer

> *Lord, search my heart. Am I holding on to anything
> or anyone I need to let go of today? I desire truth in
> the inner parts of me. I want to be obedient and live a
> life of forgiveness. Show me the practical steps in my
> own life and situations.*

Give, and it will be given to you. . . . For with the measure you use,
it will be measured to you.

Luke 6:38

■ Today I Believe . . .

It is God's will that I forgive others, letting go of offenses for the
sake of obedience to God's law of love.

Day 23

Put Down the Stones

Dare to Quit Being Critical of Others

Anyone who does not do what is
right is not a child of God; neither
is anyone who does not love his
brother.

1 John 3:10

Jesus—compassionate, loving, always looking for the best in people. He was quick to love, kind in correction, strong in conviction, and humble in his dealings with people. I like to think of this as the Jesus style of life: loving others. But the problem with loving others is that I am often critical of them, don't understand their choices, and get frustrated to the point of pointing a finger in judgment. I wonder what would happen if I just laid down the stones. What if I could quit being so critical? What would life look like then?

Today's Praise/Prayer: Psalm 61

Hear my cry, O God;
   listen to my prayer.

From the ends of the earth I call to you,
    I call as my heart grows faint;
    lead me to the rock that is higher than I.
For you have been my refuge,
    a strong tower against the foe.
I long to dwell in your tent forever
    and take refuge in the shelter of your wings.

vv. 1–4

Today's Truth: Matthew 7:1; John 8:3–7; Romans 14:13; 1 Corinthians 13:5; 1 Thessalonians 4:11

The teachers of the law and the Pharisees brought in a woman caught in adultery. They made her stand before the group and said to Jesus, "Teacher, this woman was caught in the act of adultery. In the Law Moses commanded us to stone such women. Now what do you say?" They were using this question as a trap, in order to have a basis for accusing him. But Jesus bent down and started to write on the ground with his finger. When they kept on questioning him, he straightened up and said to them, "If any one of you is without sin, let him be the first to throw a stone at her."

John 8:3–7

Let's examine this Scripture passage first and then go back to the others in a moment.

You might know the story. It's familiar, but it doesn't change us because we usually don't apply it to our lives. Jesus was in the temple courts teaching. People gathered around him, and the Pharisees tried to trick him in front of the crowd. Now before we get to today's truth, keep in mind that the Pharisees were the religious leaders of the day, the ones who seemingly had it together. Jesus spoke to the Pharisees, and when he did, he was speaking to religious God folk, not run-of-the-mill nonbelievers. His message to the Pharisees has meaning for us today too.

The Message states it like this, "The sinless one among you, go first: Throw the stone."

I don't know about you, but the last time I checked, I was certainly *not* sinless. Yet, as I search my heart, I can recall hectic stone-throwing days. The throws may have taken place in my mind, but that didn't make the judgments any less real. When I judge others, I am walking further away from living like Jesus and drawing closer to doing things in my own way.

Here are the other verses to ponder:

Do not judge, or you too will be judged.

Matthew 7:1

Don't criticize.

Matthew 7:1 Phillips

Let us no longer criticize one another.

Romans 14:13 AMP

Love [God's love/*agape*] does not keep track of other people's wrongs.

1 Corinthians 13:5 AMP

Mind your own business.

1 Thessalonians 4:11 Message

I am convicted. Most women are critical. It is a habit we develop as little girls and carry with us into our adult lives. Our critical nature usually comes from our own insecurity or our need to control other people. But since it comes from our hearts, it is not innocent. When we are critical, we are not a reflection of Christ. If Christ is living in us, we should view people as Christ does, not with the average critical thoughts we play around with.

Dale Carnegie said, "Any fool can criticize, condemn, and complain. . . . But it takes character and self-control to be understanding and forgiving."[1]

A critical spirit can keep us stuck. When we are filled with the negative, there isn't much room for the positive. Criticism is not the way of *agape* and not the way to follow after Christ.

I am concerned that I have been a Christian for so long and have not been overly concerned about my stone throwing, either in attitude or in action. I too can be much like a Pharisee. I look good in service and actions on the outside, while inside I am filled with criticisms. I judge others because they don't do things the way I might do them. How arrogant! Yes, now I am concerned about that. So in a practical sense, how do we go about laying down the stones?

Here is a list based on Romans 12:9–18 from the Message:

- Love from the center of who you are.
- Run from evil and hold on to good.
- Practice playing second fiddle.
- Bless your enemies; no cursing under your breath.
- Get along with each other.
- Don't be stuck up.
- Don't hit back.
- Discover the beauty in everyone.
- Don't insist on getting even.
- Don't let evil get the best of you; get the best of evil by doing good.

Today's Dare: Quit Being Critical of Others

- Identify the last time you threw stones at someone.
- Ask God to forgive you.
- Look for good in that person and begin to acknowledge the good.

- Ask God to show you each time you begin to judge or criticize someone today.
- Stop yourself and just say no to the stones of criticism or judgment.
- Put a rock or stone in a prominent place to remind you not to throw stones at other people.

Journal

Acknowledging where we are is the first step to living in faith and truth.

Today's truth is speaking to me . . .

_____
_____
_____
_____
_____
_____
_____

God is asking me to . . .

_____
_____
_____
_____
_____
_____
_____

My challenge is to . . .

_____
_____
_____

Today's Prayer

Lord, I need you. My human flesh is so strong, my stone-throwing arm too well developed. Help me, Jesus. Take truth to the very core of me, convicting me, instructing me, and changing me.

Do not judge, and you will not be judged. Do not condemn, and you will not be condemned. . . . For with the measure you use, it will be measured to you.

Luke 6:37–38

Today I Believe . . .

The way I treat others will come back to me.

189

Day 24

Practice the Presence of People

*Dare to Allow Your Heart to Connect
and Your Mind to Engage with Others*

How good and pleasant it is
when brothers live together in
unity!

Psalm 133:1

Connie was getting increasingly edgy and depressed. She was iso-
lating herself, and she knew it. It seemed she didn't have the time,
energy, or power to stop it.

"I am so lonely," Connie said in tears. "But I don't have any
time to add one more thing to my life. I know it's a problem, but
I guess I will just have to deal with it because it's not changing
anytime soon."

I knew what she was talking about. For about a seven-year stretch
of my life, it seemed I had no time for people. It seems funny to
say that now, but it was my reality—a reality that led me to a very
dry, sad place. Looking back, I realize there could have been time. I
was just not placing value on people and instead was putting value

190

on all the things I had to do and the responsibilities in front of me. I learned the hard way that God created us for relationship not just with him but with others as well. We were created to connect, to do life together, to bear each others' burdens, to care with our whole being for those whom Christ loves.

Honoring the value of people is a choice we make when we dare to live the Jesus style of life. He loved people, walked with them, ate with them, processed with them, directed them, cried with them, healed them, gave to them, and forgave them. I want to learn to value people the way Jesus did.

■ Today's Praise/Prayer: Psalm 15

> LORD, who may dwell in your sanctuary?
>   Who may live on your holy hill?
> He whose walk is blameless
>   and who does what is righteous,
> who speaks the truth from his heart
>   and has no slander on his tongue,
> who does his neighbor no wrong
>   and casts no slur on his fellow man.

vv. 1–3

■ Today's Truth: Romans 12:9–10, 15–16

Love must be sincere. Hate what is evil; cling to what is good. Be devoted to one another in brotherly love. Honor one another above yourselves. . . . Rejoice with those who rejoice; mourn with those who mourn. Live in harmony with one another. Do not be proud, but be willing to associate with people of low position. Do not be conceited.

Romans 12:9–10, 15–16

What is sincere love? Let's face it, the value of love has become watered down in the society we live in. We love chocolate, our favorite color, our favorite store, and other people. It's no wonder we don't realize the impact of love when it is spoken of in Scripture.

God's love is different. It is pure and not self-seeking; it is patient and kind; it always believes the best in another; it doesn't fail. So, that said, it's easy to see how we need his love if we are ever going to connect with others in a way that brings healthy relationships. Without the love of God, we are left to our selfish selves. And, all of us know that being "her" is often not a pretty picture. On the other side of that is the "us" that has been created in Christ Jesus for good works, and yes . . . good relationships. Just look at what the Romans passage tells us is Jesus's style of loving and living in relationship with others:

- Do you see any good? Cling to what is good!
- Are you an island unto yourself? Be devoted to other people!
- Do you live in a critical spirit toward others? God says we are to honor not criticize!
- Jealous of others' accomplishments or blessings? God can give you the heart to rejoice with them!
- Is pride a problem? God's way is to honor others and associate with all people!

■ Today's Dare: Allow Your Heart to Connect and Your Mind to Engage with Others

- Dare to watch for needs around you and see what you can do to meet them.
- Invite someone over to dinner, out to coffee, or to a movie, even if it makes you uncomfortable.
- Join a small group at your church or school.
- Make people a priority.

- Listen to the person who is talking to you. Stay focused on that person for that moment. Give her your full mind and attention.
- Be happy when others succeed. Block jealousy from your life by committing your life to God and trusting his outcome for you.

Journal

Acknowledging where we are is the first step to living in faith and truth.

Today's truth is speaking to me . . .

_____

_____

_____

_____

_____

God is asking me to . . .

_____

_____

_____

_____

_____

My challenge is to . . .

_____

_____

_____

_____

Today's Prayer

Lord, I do not want to live a self-absorbed life, nor do I want to live behind self-protective walls and barriers. Teach me how to love others in an authentic way that enriches their lives and honors you. Father, lead me into relationships that are your choice for me and to friends who are part of your design for my life.

A man of many companions may come to ruin,
but there is a friend who sticks closer than a brother.

Proverbs 18:24

Today I Believe . . .

People matter to God. I will be open to others and to the relationships God has for me.

Day 25

The Power of Words

*Dare to Use Your Tongue to Bless
and Build Up Others*

A word fitly spoken is like apples of
gold in pictures of silver.

Proverbs 25:11 KJV

I grew up with the saying, "Sticks and stones can break my bones, but words will never hurt me." I also grew up confused as to why words cut so deep and hurt so long. Truth is, trigger words can still threaten my peace and quickly alter my attitude. Yes, words hurt. We all need to realize that our words can deeply wound others. Things we say can start so innocently and end so terribly. Gossip, negative comments, condescending attitudes all are things that tear others down.

Today we are going to focus on our words. Take inventory of how you usually speak to others. Become accountable to God for your mouth, and get excited about the flip side of the negative— the positive effect uplifting words can have.

■ Today's Praise/Prayer: Psalm 37

> Do not fret because of evil men
>> or be envious of those who do wrong;
> for like the grass they will soon wither,
>> like green plants they will soon die away.
> Trust in the LORD and do good;
>> dwell in the land and enjoy safe pasture.
> Delight yourself in the LORD
>> and he will give you the desires of your heart.
>
> vv. 1–4

■ Today's Truth: Proverbs 10:19; 12:18; 16:21; 18:8; Ecclesiastes 10:12; Ephesians 5:19; James 1:19

> When words are many, sin is not absent,
>> but he who holds his tongue is wise.
>
> Proverbs 10:19

> Reckless words pierce like a sword,
>> but the tongue of the wise brings healing.
>
> Proverbs 12:18

> The wise in heart are called discerning,
>> and pleasant words promote instruction.
>
> Proverbs 16:21

> The words of a gossip are like choice morsels;
>> they go down to a man's inmost parts.
>
> Proverbs 18:8

> Words from a wise man's mouth are gracious,
>> but a fool is consumed by his own lips.
>
> Ecclesiastes 10:12

196

Speak to one another with psalms, hymns and spiritual songs. Sing and make music in your heart to the Lord.

Ephesians 5:19

My dear brothers, take note of this: Everyone should be quick to listen, slow to speak and slow to become angry.

James 1:19

I have a friend who is going to counseling for mouth management. I am so proud of her. There came a point when she realized that her foot was always in her mouth and that blurting things out was hurting people she didn't want to hurt. And while managing our mouth is important, keep in mind that it is out of the heart the mouth speaks. So heart and mouth go hand in hand.

These verses speak for themselves, don't they? James 1:19 in particular is one we should commit to memory, as it is so contrary to how most of us interact with others.

- Be quick to listen.
- Be slow to speak.
- Be slow to become angry.

Today's Dare: Use Your Tongue to Bless and Build Up Others

- Pay attention to what comes out of your mouth.
- Watch for gossip and refuse to converse in a negative fashion about anyone.
- Look at your heart attitude, as that is what prompts what you say.
- Look for ways to turn a negative conversation into a positive one. When someone says something negative about someone, counter with something that is more pleasant.

- Find words of encouragement to give to people in your life. Realize that when you encourage you are giving out courage for people to continue on the journey of life.
- Dare to listen more and speak less.

Journal

Acknowledging where we are is the first step to living in faith and truth.

Today's truth is speaking to me . . .

_____

_____

_____

_____

_____

_____

God is asking me to . . .

_____

_____

_____

_____

_____

My challenge is to . . .

_____

_____

_____

_____

Today's Prayer

Father, I come to you with my mouth. Teach me how to manage it. It is an instrument of cursing or blessing, and I desire it to honor you, blessing you and others. Give me encouraging words and warn me when conversations are getting to a place of gossip and dishonor. I desire, in this most practical area, to love you by loving others.

> Pleasant words are a honeycomb,
>> sweet to the soul and healing to the bones.
>>> Proverbs 16:24

Today I Believe . . .

Pleasant words are healing, and I will seek opportunities to use them to give others courage to face the day.

Day 26

The Humble Heart

*Dare to Walk in Humility
and Grace toward Others*

Comfort, Comfort my people, says
your God.

Isaiah 40:1

Have you ever known anyone who was especially aloof or who seemed arrogant? What kind of effect did that arrogant attitude have on you? If people matter to God, it's no wonder we are instructed over and over to put others before ourselves, humbling ourselves in the process. This kind of living is difficult and unnatural, and not many people do it. In fact, in our me-first society, putting others above ourselves is often unheard of.

God has a better way. Humility involves shadowing the life and nature of Christ. We need a humble heart if we are going to live in love toward others and if we are interested in honoring Christ.

■ Today's Praise/Prayer: Psalm 23

> You prepare a table before me
> in the presence of my enemies.
> You anoint my head with oil;
> my cup overflows.
> Surely goodness and love will follow me
> all the days of my life.

vv. 5–6

■ Today's Truth: Romans 8:5; Philippians 2:5–8; 1 Peter 5:5–7

Those who live according to the sinful nature have their minds set on what that nature desires; but those who live in accordance with the Spirit have their minds set on what the Spirit desires.

Romans 8:5

Your attitude should be the same as that of Christ Jesus:
> Who, being in very nature God,
> did not consider equality with God something to be grasped,
> but made himself nothing,
> taking the very nature of a servant,
> being made in human likeness.
> And being found in appearance as a man,
> he humbled himself
> and became obedient to death.

Philippians 2:5–8

Clothe yourselves with humility toward one another, because, "God opposes the proud but gives grace to the humble." Humble yourselves, therefore, under God's mighty hand, that he may lift you up in due time. Cast all your anxiety on him because he cares for you.

1 Peter 5:5–7

201

God opposes us when we walk in pride. I don't want that kind of relationship with God. I want a relationship of grace, intimacy, and connectedness. For that to happen, I must humble myself before him daily.

Humility does not mean lying down on the ground while everyone walks over you. Humility is a life submitted to God. Humility is saying to our Father, "You are God and I am not!" Walking in humility toward others is not that difficult to understand; it is simply putting them first.

Whoa! Not so simple, right? Why? Because we are selfish by human nature. But part of the faith dare is allowing God to shape us according to the new spiritual nature we have inherited in Christ. And that nature is humble and loving. Christ gave us an example of humility by dying for people who didn't care, were in their sins, were undeserving.

It is this same attitude that we are to carry through life. Rather than feeling entitled to receive, we need to be freed to give.

Note that after telling us to be humble, 1 Peter tells us to give our cares to God. A woman who has properly placed her cares in God's hands has more space in her mind and heart to humbly love others.

■ Today's Dare: Walk in Humility and Grace toward Others

- Humble yourself in attitude and action.
- If you have the opportunity today to overlook an offense, do it.
- Practice saying the word *whatever* and incorporate it into your lifestyle.
- Think of ways you can be more flexible, less demanding.
- In relating with the people you work with or live with, try to fix your mind on their needs rather than your own.
- Today challenge yourself to get out of self and actively look for the needs of others and listen to the opinions of others before inserting your own.

Journal

Acknowledging where we are is the first step to living in faith and truth.

Today's truth is speaking to me . . .

_____

_____

_____

_____

_____

_____

_____

God is asking me to . . .

_____

_____

_____

_____

_____

My challenge is to . . .

_____

_____

_____

_____

Today's Prayer

Lord, teach me your way. Show me how to walk as you walked, love as you loved, live as you lived— humbly obedient and yielded.

Be self-controlled and alert. Your enemy the devil prowls around like a roaring lion looking for someone to devour.

1 Peter 5:8

Today I Believe . . .

God desires me to clothe myself in humility and resist the devil by resisting pride.

Day 27

Measure Out Goodness

*Dare to Be Generous in Love
and Practical Kindness*

> But just as you excel in everything—in
> faith, in speech, in knowledge, in
> complete earnestness and in your
> love for us—see that you also excel
> in this grace of giving.
>
> 2 Corinthians 8:7

Life is filled with ordinary days. Most people go about their day, doing their own thing and minding their own business. Not Pauline. Every day she thought of ways to bless people and lived out her faith by finding practical solutions that helped friends and neighbors in need. I was lucky enough to be one of her neighbors.

During a rough time in my life, as I was reeling from the pain of a marital breakup, Pauline found ways to help me with my children. She offered to take them off my hands for a while each day, but she did more than just take them off my hands. She found ways to make them feel loved and did things to let them know they had a place to belong.

Pauline was on a mission. She spent a few Saturday mornings at garage sales buying boys' toys—cars, trucks, and action figures. Before long she had turned her garage into a play haven for two little boys hurting from their parents' split. She bought an old dresser and filled each drawer with a different type of activity—from games to Play-Doh to matchbox cars. That old dresser welcomed my children, offering them things to do, making them feel special. My kids thought this was great fun and began looking forward to going across the street to Pauline's house.

She also let the boys help her put together meals. When they were done cooking, they would proudly bring dinner home to me. As if this was not enough, she even included their height measurements on the same wall that marked her own grandchildren's growth. Just a little extra effort on her part made a huge difference in my young sons' lives. As adults they still smile when speaking of Pauline. We will never forget her—she demonstrated a kindness and practical love that blessed our lives forever.

God calls us to this kind of kindness, this type of giving, and this type of love.

■ Today's Praise/Prayer: Psalm 41

> Blessed is he who has regard for the weak;
>> the LORD delivers him in times of trouble.
> The LORD will protect him and preserve his life;
>> he will bless him in the land
>> and not surrender him to the desire of his foes.

vv. 1–2

■ Today's Truth: Luke 6:38; Galatians 6:7, 9–10

Give, and it will be given to you. A good measure, pressed down, shaken together and running over, will be poured into your lap. For with the measure you use, it will be measured to you.

Luke 6:38

Do not be deceived: God cannot be mocked. A man reaps what he sows. . . . Let us not become weary in doing good, for at the proper time we will reap a harvest if we do not give up. Therefore, as we have opportunity, let us do good to all people, especially to those who belong to the family of believers.

Galatians 6:7, 9–10

It is easy to think of lofty ideas of love, grace, forgiveness . . . and yes, giving. And, all would be easy to do if we only had to come up with heady theories and ideas. But if we are to live in faith and be all that God has made us to be, we must also embrace the truth that because God is generous in Spirit, we too are to be conformed into his image as givers, generous with our time, hearts, money, concern—and everything else that makes up life. Take a look at the breakdown of Scripture for practical application.

- Giving is a biblical principle.
- The way we give will be measured back to us.
- When we give a good measure, we receive back more than we gave in the first place.
- We reap what we sow in relationships.
- We are to keep focused on loving others, giving freely, and doing good. Do not grow weary!
- Every opportunity to do good is a God-sized opportunity.

◾ Today's Dare: Be Generous in Love and Practical Kindness

- Make a list of the people God has placed in your life—relatives, neighbors, co-workers, church members, etc.
- Who on that list is going through something and needs to be blessed by love?
- What practical things would meet their need?
- How can you gather resources to help them?

- Jot down some generic ways to bless other people, just to get you thinking about how you can give to others when given the opportunity.
- Think of an act of kindness that blessed you in the past. Why did that act bless you? How can you follow the example of the person who was a blessing in your life?

Journal

Acknowledging where we are is the first step to living in faith and truth.

Today's truth is speaking to me . . .

_____

_____

_____

_____

_____

_____

God is asking me to . . .

_____

_____

_____

_____

_____

_____

My challenge is to . . .

_____

_____

_____

_____

_____

_____

Today's Prayer

Forgive me for focusing on my own needs more than on the needs of others. Open my eyes and my heart to needs around me and give me a willingness to do what I can to love others in practical ways. Make me a giver and give me a generous heart and spirit.

Keep on loving each other as brothers. Do not forget to entertain strangers, for by so doing some people have entertained angels without knowing it.

Hebrews 13:1–2

Today I Believe . . .

It is God's good plan for me to bless others, give to others, and find ways to show God's love in tangible ways to the people in my life.

Day 28

Live Unselfishly

Dare to Seek Another's Best

> But encourage one another daily, as
> long as it is called Today, so that
> none of you may be hardened by
> sin's deceitfulness.
>
> Hebrews 3:13

Less of me and more of thee . . . this is one hard prayer! It's easy
to pray it, but when the evidence that God is answering this prayer
starts kicking in, it becomes the hardest thing ever prayed. Why?
Because praying for less of me is in essence praying for the stripping
of self. And, quite frankly, though I want this stripping, this type
of stripping is difficult. This type of stripping leaves me vulnerable
and feeling naked!

A stripping of selfishness seems to hit most in our relationships
with other people. God created us for relationship, so it makes
sense that he strips us and changes us the most while we are in
relationship. I think it would be easy to follow the way of love if
I was in a cave by myself. I could come up with great theory and

live large in my head with thoughts and words of love . . . blah, blah, blah . . . until my neighbor in the next cave comes to borrow some sugar. Can't she manage her own shopping list? She's always out of something. Yes, when it comes to real life and practical love, less of me and more of thee is *the* necessary prayer!

I live in a world with people, and so do you. People who rub us the wrong way, hurt us, push every last button. You know what I'm talking about . . . real life, real relationships, real people. We do need a real God and the power of his love. We also need some practical instruction.

■ Today's Praise/Prayer: Psalm 25

> Remember, O LORD, your great mercy and love,
>   for they are from of old.
> Remember not the sins of my youth
>   and my rebellious ways;
> according to your love remember me,
>   for you are good, O LORD.
> Good and upright is the LORD;
>   therefore he instructs sinners in his ways.
> He guides the humble in what is right
>   and teaches them his way.
> All the ways of the LORD are loving and faithful.

vv. 6–10

■ Today's Truth: Luke 6:27–31

Love your enemies, do good to those who hate you, bless those who curse you, pray for those who mistreat you. If someone strikes you on one cheek, turn to him the other also. If someone takes your cloak, do not stop him from taking your tunic. Give to everyone who asks you, and if anyone takes what belongs to you, do not demand it back. Do to others as you would have them do to you.

Luke 6:27–31

There are people who don't like us . . . even hate us. There are people who feel like foe, not friend. What should we do?

- Love them. Let God's love flow through you to them.
- Do good to them. This takes action.
- Bless them. Speak kindly of them and to them.
- Pray for them. Speak to the Father about them and for them.
- Give to them. Sow seeds of kindness.

Do to them what you would want them to do to you.

■ Today's Dare: Seek Another's Best

- Is there someone in your life who keeps hurting you? What would turning the other cheek look like in that relationship?
- Today practice speaking kindly and speaking words that will bless others.
- Pray for those who have hurt you and ask God to bless them.
- Find something good you can do for someone who hurt you.
- In a perfect world, how would you like to be treated? Now go and treat others the way you wish people treated you.
- Imagine the kindest person you know—duplicate that kindness!

■ Journal

Acknowledging where we are is the first step to living in faith and truth.

Today's truth is speaking to me . . .

_____

_____

_____

_____

_____

_____

_____

_____

God is asking me to . . .

_____

_____

_____

_____

_____

_____

My challenge is to . . .

_____

_____

_____

_____

_____

Today's Prayer

Father, I cannot live in your love without you in me doing it. I ask you to teach me to live in you in such a way as to lose myself in your love, your way, your life. I desire to follow you, paying attention to your words to the disciples so many years ago. I hear you. Now help me obey you. Obedience is the wild part of this journey. I want to be that kind of wild!

I am sending him to you for this very purpose, that you may know how we are, and that he may encourage you.

Ephesians 6:22

Today I Believe . . .

I need to quit being selfish and be open to God when he sends me out to encourage and bless someone else.

Day 29

Having All We Need

Dare to Choose Contentment in Your Relationships

Your heavenly Father knows that you
need them.

Matthew 6:32

Every woman lives in a tent—con*tent* or discon*tent*! Our attitude affects our relationships with other people. Because of this, we should pay close attention to our attitude. When we are content, we are free to love and care for others as Jesus has called us to do. When we are discontent, we are constantly critical, and this affects everyone around us. Before long, every relationship is tainted with the negative. Each of us can turn this around by making a choice—a daily choice to dwell in gratitude in our circumstances and relationships.

I like the story about the guy who went to the pet store to get a singing parakeet. He was a bachelor, and his house was quiet.

He hoped a singing bird would make it a little more like home. The pet store owner had just the bird for him, so he bought it and took the bird home.

The next day the bachelor came home from work to a house full of music. He went to the cage to feed the bird and noticed for the first time that the parakeet had only one leg. He felt ripped off and called the store to complain about being sold a one-legged bird.

"What do you want," the store owner responded, "a bird who can sing or a bird who can dance?"

This is a good story for all of us who are disappointed with people or things in our life right now. It is all in how we view things.

■ Today's Praise/Prayer: Psalm 18

As for God, his way is perfect;
   the word of the LORD is flawless.
He is a shield
   for all who take refuge in him.
For who is God besides the LORD?
   And who is the Rock except our God?
It is God who arms me with strength
   and makes my way perfect.
He makes my feet like the feet of a deer;
   he enables me to stand on the heights. . . .
You give me your shield of victory,
   and your right hand sustains me.

vv. 30–33, 35

■ Today's Truth: Philippians 4:4–8, 11–13, 19

Rejoice in the Lord always. I will say it again: Rejoice! . . . The Lord is near. Do not be anxious about anything, but in everything, by prayer and petition, with thanksgiving, present your requests to God. And the peace of God, which transcends all understanding, will guard your hearts and your minds in Christ Jesus. Finally, brothers, whatever is true, whatever is noble, whatever is right, whatever is pure, whatever is lovely, whatever is admirable—if anything is excellent or praiseworthy—think about such things.

Philippians 4:4–8

I have learned to be content whatever the circumstances. I know what it is to be in need, and I know what it is to have plenty. I have learned the secret of being content in any and every situation. . . . I can do everything through him who gives me strength.

Philippians 4:11–13

And my God will meet all your needs according to his glorious riches in Christ Jesus.

Philippians 4:19

Just today I stumbled into a place of discontentment and neediness. A hurt from someone in my past came and slapped me in the face. I didn't like the sting but easily brushed it off. But during the day thoughts of the past hurt kept creeping into my mind. Before I realized it I was driving down the street with tears pouring down my face. How can something that happened so long ago still hurt today? How can I go from positive to negative in such a short span of time?

Maybe you know what I mean.

A few months ago I cut my finger. I should have gotten stitches, but I didn't want to miss my stepdaughter's graduation. So I bandaged it tightly and went on with life. In time the cut healed, scarred, and the finger went back to normal. That is until something bumps it too hard or brushes against it the wrong way . . . then it zings! A reminder of the injury is always just a bump away. Healed? Yes! Completely gone? No.

I was divorced by a husband who no longer loved me. The pain of what happened was intense. I thought I would never get over it. Even after remarriage, the pain of my past clung to me for years.

217

And just when I thought it was gone for good . . . bump . . . Zing! Zing! Zing! Tears.

Was I crying tears over my ex-husband? No. But I was crying over broken places in my heart. I was crying because sometimes life is filled with disappointments. Over the years I have had to learn to focus on God in the middle of my life dramas and traumas! The focus has saved me and revamped my expectations.

I don't expect never to experience pain or disappointment again, but I do expect God to teach me through the pain and help me over the hump when the pain resurfaces. I trust Jesus to do in me what I cannot do for myself. The key is our focus when these things happen. Our focus in life has a huge impact on our relationships with other people. In fact, it might be more important than anything a person does or says to us. Our viewpoint sets the course. Philippians teaches us to do some important things.

- Refuse to worry about circumstances or need.
- Pray instead, giving your current need or relational struggle to God.
- Receive his peace.
- Look for good and dwell there.
- Continually look for the good in every person you know.
- Practice finding the good in people and dwell on the good parts.
- Live in contentment and strength.
- Look to God to supply all your needs according to his supply.

▪ Today's Dare: Choose Contentment in Your Relationships

- Think about the person who usually drives you up a wall. What would be different if you had a different attitude?

- Try to find good in that person and act out of the good you see.
- Practice dwelling on that person's good qualities.
- Speak positively about that person.
- Trust that God will give you everything you need to live in contentment and peace with all people.
- When an old hurt resurfaces, run to God, give it to him in prayer, thank him that he is good!

Journal

Acknowledging where we are is the first step to living in faith and truth.

Today's truth is speaking to me . . .

_____

_____

_____

_____

_____

_____

_____

God is asking me to . . .

_____

_____

_____

_____

_____

_____

_____

My challenge is to . . .

_____

_____

_____

_____

_____

■ Today's Prayer

> *Lord, you are perfect, and I put my trust in you. I am learning that my disappointment can be used as your appointment for personal growth, shaping, and maturing. May your will be done in the story of my life. You supply my every need—physical, material, emotional, spiritual. Thank you.*

My God will supply all your needs according to his glorious riches in Christ Jesus.

Philippians 4:19

■ Today I Believe . . .

God is aware of my need for his strength to be accepting of and content with people who are different from me, upset me, annoy me, or otherwise push my buttons.

Day 30

When It Depends on You

Dare to Be the First One to Change

Do not be overcome by evil, but
overcome evil with good.

Romans 12:21

The frustrated look on their faces said it all. They were stuck in an emotional deadlock—neither one wanting to give in. I carefully said, "Someone is going to have to make a move. Something has got to give."

The angry wife burst out in tears. "Why do I have to be the first one to change?" At that point I was reminded of something author Nancy Missler says: "Because your spiritual life depends on it!"

We all want our way; that's nothing new. This month of daring ourselves to live differently has been about laying ourselves down in order to learn to walk as a Christ follower. Each day we have been challenged by God's Word. We have undoubtedly not liked some of what we have been dared to do, but that's to be expected. We want our way, want to be right, want to win the fight, and want to be in control. Unfortunately, when we live like this, the life and love of Christ do not flow out of us as they should. When we are empty spiritually, we have nothing left to give. The Christian life is about being filled with the Spirit and operating from that place. And if that's the case, then why shouldn't we be the first to make a move toward change?

Today's Praise/Prayer: Psalm 141

> Set a guard over my mouth, O LORD;
> keep watch over the door of my lips.
> Let not my heart be drawn to what is evil,
> to take part in wicked deeds
> with men who are evildoers;
> let me not eat of their delicacies.
> Let a righteous man strike me—it is a kindness;
> let him rebuke me—it is oil on my head.
> My head will not refuse it.

vv. 3–5

Today's Truth: Romans 12:18–21

If it is possible, as far as it depends on you, live at peace with everyone. Do not take revenge, my friends, but leave room for God's wrath, for it is written: "It is mine to avenge; I will repay," says the Lord. On the contrary:

> "If your enemy is hungry, feed him;
> if he is thirsty, give him something to drink.
> In doing this, you will heap burning coals on his head."
> Do not be overcome by evil, but overcome evil with good.

Romans 12:18–21

Sometimes it is not possible to make peace. Often others refuse it. But that refusal doesn't get us off the hook. We must do our part, make the first move, do what would bring peace and healing in the relationship. *The Faith Dare* began with "The Miracle of a New Heart," surrendering our hearts to God. And now we end with the same. We need to surrender our hearts, attitudes, and words to God in practical ways—practical ways that will stretch us, even when our pride does not want it. Especially then. In fact, those times are the perfect opportunity to reject our desire and choose God's. You will find, more often than not, that if you make the first move, things will improve. There is a reason this idea is in Scripture.

Take out a pitcher from your cupboard. Look at it, think of its purpose, and then fill it with water. Now slowly pour that water down the sink. Watch it leave the pitcher. Once empty, can the pitcher pour out anymore? Neither can we. We must be filled in order to be used by God. Second Timothy 2:20–25 speaks of us as being instruments for noble purposes, useful to the Master, prepared to do any good work. To be that instrument we must:

- flee evil desires of youth
- pursue righteousness, faith, love, and peace
- have nothing to do with stupid arguments
- be kind to everyone
- not be resentful
- gently instruct others in hope

As we end, then, let's pray the prayer of David from Psalm 139:23–24:

> Search me, O God, and know my heart;
>   test me and know my anxious thoughts.
> See if there is any offensive way in me,
>   and lead me in the way everlasting.

- Search me.
- Cleanse me.
- Fill me.
- Use me.

Pray the above passage. Allow God to show you what he is cleansing from you that is unloving toward others in attitude or action.

Today's Dare: Be the First One to Change

- Commit, or entrust, to God the details of your life and your day . . . the practical stuff.
- Dare to do what you can in each situation you face.
- Ask God to forgive stubbornness and pride and the desire to push away from people.
- Take steps in the direction of peace.
- Focus each day on being his instrument.
- Ask God to use you. Look for ways to bless others.

> Whatever our hands touch—we leave fingerprints!
> On walls, on furniture, on doorknobs, dishes, books,
> There's no escape.
> As we touch we leave our identity.
> O God, wherever I go today
> Help me leave your heartprints!
> Heartprints of compassion, of understanding and love.[1]

Journal

Acknowledging where we are is the first step to living in faith and truth.

Today's truth is speaking to me . . .

_____
_____
_____
_____
_____
_____
_____

God is asking me to . . .

_____

_____

_____

_____

_____

_____

My challenge is to . . .

_____

_____

_____

_____

_____

Today's Prayer

*Lord, I want all that you have for me. I realize that
to honor you means that I must be open to allowing
you to flow through me with your love and care for
others. I desire to be your touch in this world that I
live in. Make my life a heartprint of your most Holy
Spirit and a reflection of your pure and unselfish love
for others. Do in me what I cannot do on my own.*

> Delight yourself in the LORD
> and he will give you the desires of your heart.
>
> Psalm 37:4

Today I Believe . . .

God will provide my heart's desire and every need. Through him I
can live up, delighting in God; live in, surrendered to his love; and
live out, showing that love to others.

Conclusion

Moving Forward and Trusting God

Set your mind on things above, not on earthly things.
For you died and your life is now hidden with Christ
in God.

Colossians 3:2–3

You did it! It takes thirty days to form a new habit. During the past thirty days, you began the formation of a new habit of seeking God, processing truth, and finding ways to live out God's Word. You also practiced dying to self by choosing the right things—ways of doing life that are biblical but might be uncomfortable.

Our best, fullest life becomes ours as we focus not on self but on Christ and his ways for us. It is amazing how making this change, even for a day, can make such a huge difference in attitude and action. But as you move forward, you can be certain of one thing: there is an enemy lurking about trying to rob you of your faith. You must purchase a security system and install it on your life. The security system is joy. To install it you must remove your previous system of fear, worry, and doubt. Once you change service providers, your life will be different, safer, more peaceful, and fuller. You have to make a decision to change. The offer is open to you, but you have to choose the new provider.

When we do something repeatedly, it becomes a habit. When a habit is done repeatedly and well and is producing something good, it becomes the art in which we live.

I want to develop the art of looking up. I want to make a habit of intentionally choosing my focus. I want that focus to be on Jesus Christ, who he is, how faithful he is, who I am in him. I want to surrender to his plan. I want to look up.

None of this comes naturally to us. Instead, I usually focus on how bad things are, how impossible they seem, how I never seem to be enough, how much I really want my own way.

- What is going wrong in your life today? Look up.
- What is your greatest current challenge? Look up.
- What is hurting your feelings? Look up.
- What is breaking your heart? Look up.
- What is causing you pain? Look up.

Your life is no longer your own. Your life is not random. It is hidden in Christ. You are protected, shielded, cared for, provided for . . . by Christ. You are covered by his faithfulness and power. To look up, focus your attention on what is biblically true rather than on what you are feeling.

In the moment of stress, pain, or doubt . . . stop. Choose instead to tell yourself what is true about you, your life in Christ, and God's love and faithfulness. Take a new position, stand firm in who Christ is and who you are in him. Look up! Look to him! Choose to believe. It starts as a choice, when repeated becomes a new habit, and over time becomes an art. I think looking up has become a lost art in a world in which we look to self, get discouraged, depressed, and defeated. There is a better way, and it starts with the choice to look up!

Today choose to walk in a new life.

1. Start a new morning habit. When you look at yourself in the mirror, thank God for the truth. Say to him, "Thank you, Lord, that I am alive in you. Thank you for the gift of salvation. I am your work, and you have prepared good works for me to do today, as I live to honor you."

2. Make a list of attitudes you still carry around and live in, attitudes that have always been a part of you. Recognize that Christ can give you new attitudes.

3. Get a small gift box. Wrap it up beautifully and place it where you will see it frequently during the next few weeks. Each time you see it, tell yourself the truth. "God's gift to me is Jesus. In Jesus Christ I have all I need. God has gifted me to be part of his plan."

And remember, acknowledging where we are is the first step to living in faith and truth.

We can learn a lot from the apostle Paul. Paul gives us some important keys to continuing in the faith and not losing heart as we follow God. We must see our weaknesses as a means by which God perfects his strength in us. In our weakness he receives all the glory when he moves through us with his power. We must learn to live by faith and not by what we can see with our eyes. We must remember that Christ's grace is sufficient in *all* situations.

Faith Steps

- Do not give up.
- Do not allow discouragement to have its way with you; fight it with biblical truth.

- Set your focus on faith in God. He will be faithful to the end!
- Thank God that strength and ability are not the criteria by which he chooses to use people.
- Thank God that his grace renews you daily.
- Refuse to lose heart. Instead, focus on the truth: the Lord loves you enough to change you, work in you, and have his way with you.

Closing Dares

- Take time to come up with your own plan to continue your walk of faith.
- Make adjustments in your life so as to make a habit of seeking God and focusing on him.
- Make three relationships a priority: live up to God; live in, surrendering self; live out in love toward others.

Today is just the beginning of a life of basic faith, one truth at a time, one choice at a time, and one day at a time.

I pray for you to experience God's love and presence on the journey! And I pray that all of us can learn to challenge ourselves daily—dare to follow after a God who cannot be boxed up and figured out, a God who calls us to follow him on a journey of love, peace, joy, and real life change. Here's to life!

Notes

Introduction

1. Oswald Chambers, in David McCasland's *The Quotable Oswald Chambers* (Grand Rapids: Discovery House, 2008).
2. See http://en.wikipedia.org/wiki/Twitter.
3. See http://en.wikipedia.org/wiki/Blog.

Chapter 2

1. Dr. Bruce Wilkinson, from *The Testing of Your Faith* video series.
2. Oswald Chambers, *My Utmost for His Highest* (Grand Rapids: Discovery House, 1992), August 29.

Day 1

1. Beth Moore, *A Quick Word with Beth Moore on Breaking Free* (Nashville: B&H Publishing, 2008), devotional quotes (pages not numbered).

Day 10

1. Tommy Newberry, *The 4:8 Principle* (Carol Stream, IL: Tyndale, 2007).

Part 3

1. Chuck and Nancy Missler, *The Choice* (Coeur d'Alene, ID: Koinonia House, 2001), 27.

Day 11

1. Oswald Chambers, *My Utmost for His Highest*, May 8.

Day 14

1. Max Lucado, *Grace for the Moment* (Nashville: Thomas Nelson, 2000).

Day 18

1. Stephen Arterburn, *Reframe Your Life* (New York: FaithWords, 2007), 205.

Part 4

1. Debbie Alsdorf, *He Is My Life* (Colorado Springs: David C. Cook, 2008), 16.

Day 23

1. Dale Carnegie, *How to Win Friends and Influence People*, rev. ed. (1981, repr. New York: Simon & Schuster, 2009), 14.

Day 30

1. Ruth Harms Calking, *Lord, Could You Hurry a Little?* (Wheaton: Tyndale, 1983), 79.

Debbie Alsdorf is the author of *Deeper* and *A Different Kind of Wild*. As the founder of Design4Living Ministries, she seeks to encourage women to Live Up! in the truth of God's Word. Since 1997 she has been the director of women's ministries at Cornerstone Fellowship, where she and her team lead a vibrant women's ministry. Debbie is a biblical lay counselor and a member of the American Association of Christian Counselors. She lives in Northern California.

Stop Striving for Perfection and Start Living for Real

"Debbie beautifully teaches truth that changes a woman forever."
—**Jennifer Rothschild**, author,
Lessons I Learned in the Dark and *Self Talk, Soul Talk*

 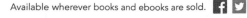

Re-energize Your Life in 90 Days

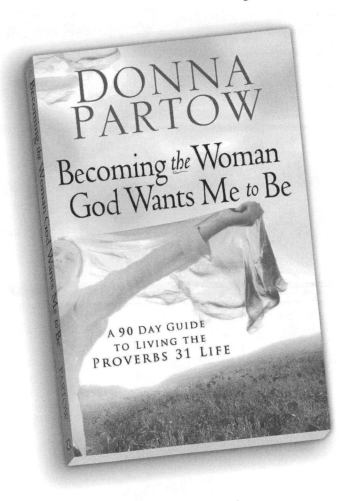

Let this powerful guide renew your energy and determination.